Italy Travel Guide: Essential Tips for First-Timers in Italy

How to Travel in Italy: Rome, Florence, Venice, Milan, Sicily and Much More

by Francesco Umbria

Table of Contents

Introduction

Italy has fascinated travelers since ancient times. Jutting out into the Mediterranean Sea, Italy seemed to naturally attract travelers and invaders alike, and most who came to this enchanted peninsula never left. Indeed, Italy is and will likely remain a popular tourist destination, in part because of the architectural remains and fascinating culture that all of these cultures left behind. In fact, Italy is unique in Europe for both the variety and the age of its monuments.

Of course, there is more to Italy than its ruins. Many are also drawn by its beaches. As a long country surrounded by the sea, it is impossible that a beach lover would not find at least one beach to fall in love with here. And because many regions of Italy are close to the sea, a beach vacation can easily be incorporated into a tour of the sites. Although many tourists may be drawn to Italy by its beaches and monuments, many find themselves most impressed by the vibrant culture and love of life of the people. For many people, the image of Italy comes as much from the films of Pier Paolo Pasolini and Lucchino Visconti as it comes from stories of Rome in the history books and tells of its beaches.

The beaches of Italy are incredible, but they are just one of many draws to Italy. And it is no surprise that Italy would be blessed with them. With over 1,000 miles of coastline, Italy has a greater number of famous beaches than most European countries, with only Spain, France, and Greece giving the Italians a run for their money. Indeed, Italy's favorable position in the Mediterranean means that many of the tourists to this land come from European countries, but that has not stopped Italy from being patronized by tourists all the world over.

Beaches would not be much of a draw if it were not for the climate. Greenland and Tierra del Fuego have beaches, too, but there are few tourists lining up to head to those places. The Italian climate is perfect for the beachgoer or anyone who has a passion for outdoor sports. This is especially true of Southern Italy where the climate may remain appropriate for beach-going and other outdoor sports even in the dead of winter.

This naturally leads to one of the most fascinating aspects of Italy: its variety. The variety in climate and geography has led to a variety of culture, too. In fact, many tourists are surprised to find that the Italian nation is host to a variety of languages, dialects, cuisines, styles of dress, and other expressions of culture. The natural division is between Northern and Southern Italy, separated by the high mountain ranges of Central Italy, but even in these two areas are there notable differences.

Northern Italy is home to Piedmont, Lombardy, Emilia-Romagna, the Veneto, and other areas each with their own language or dialect and way of life. Of course, one cannot forget Tuscany which is home to Florence, Siena, Pisa, and many other cities that have left their mark on European history because of the Italian Renaissance, humanism, and other important cultural traditions that sprung from this area. Indeed, even the language is known today as Italian sprung from the Tuscan language that originated in this influential region.

Rome and Central Italy occupy a place between Northern and Southern Italy, with features of both regions as well as traditions uniquely Roman. The reasons that tourists are drawn to Rome are obvious, with the monuments of its imperial past in varied states of ruin and preservation, but some aspects of the allure of Rome have to be experienced to be understood. In fact, this can be said of Italy in general. From the food to the ruins, to the joie de vivre of the people, Italy as a tourist nation is practically without compare in the world.

Although the marks of the Roman Empire are most felt in their capital, they can be experienced anywhere in Italy. Temples, where the Romans worshipped Jupiter, Juno, Venus, Augustus, Apollo, and Mars, can be found all over Italy and the Mediterranean region. Massive arenas that were the sites of gladiatorial combats and places where Christians were once fed to lions can also be found. Indeed, few countries have been the beneficiaries of such good marketing as Italy, with the fascination of people worldwide with the Roman emperors and gladiators serving to draw people to this land year after year.

There is more to Italy than the lure of the Romans. This is part of what makes Italy such a remarkable tourist destination. The barbarian tribes, popes, Moors, condottiere, modern Italian monarchs, and others all left their mark on this European crossroads. The remains of Northern African invasion can be found in Southern Italy, leaving its legacy in the form of peculiar cathedrals, churches, and dwellings. Even the native language of Sicily bears testament to history quite different from the rest of Italy.

Rome and Central Italy are dominated by the legacy of the Popes who ruled as independent rulers here for nearly one thousand years. Contrary to what one might imagine, the papal legacy did not render this region any less peaceful as warrior popes struggled to aggrandize this area just like everyone else with an army in Italy. One of the most famous popes was the Catalan Rodrigo Borgia, also known as Pope Alexander VI, who lived in the critical time of the beginning of the Italian Renaissance and the French invasion of Italy in the early 16th century.

It is stories like those of the Borgias, Viscontis, Sforzas, Medicis, and others which lend Italy a mystical quality. Tourists can walk the same streets that Cesare and Lucrezia Borgia walked, tour the palaces where the Medici rulers dispatched their wives and rivals in their fight for power. They can see frescoes painted by Leonardo and Michelangelo and sculptures by Raphael and Donatello all resting in tranquility in humble churches or in small piazzas.

Suffice it to say, there is much to fascinate about Italy. Indeed, a review of the history of Italy is important in order to understand how this midsize country manages to host such great variety in languages, cuisines, and architectural monuments. Your introduction to Italy will begin with a review of Italian history, going all the way back to the so-called Sea People who populated the Mediterranean before the Romans and who were likely ancestors to the Etruscans (who gave Tuscany its name).

Just as important as the review of Italian history is the survey of the geography of Italy. This will give the reader an understanding of how cultural variability sprang up in Italy: due to the mountains, rivers, and other geographical features that divide the land into distinct regions that evolved differently through the period of the Dark Ages and Early Modern period. These regions will be important in planning your trip to Italy as choosing where to visit and when is an important part of any Italian itinerary.

The reality is that there is so much to see in Italy that few are able to see it all, at least not in one trip. Planning your Italian journey thus becomes just as important as learning what the sites are to visit in Italy and why certain regions of Italy have different sorts of sites than others. Because there are others just like you planning to visit this fascinating country, concerns of when the best time to visit is and where to visit when you go will be important for you to address long before you get there.

Visiting Rome should be at the top of your list of sights to see while you are in Italy. The Roman Empire last for more than 500 years (more than one thousand if you count the later Eastern Roman or Byzantine Empire), and it left a legacy of monuments all across Western Europe and the Mediterranean region, not least of all in the city of Rome itself. Rome is filled with ancient temples, bathhouses, palaces, columns, obelisks, and other monuments that attest to a civilization that even today represents the benchmark to which other civilizations are prepared.

Any tourist to Rome can easily get lost in not only the sea of ancient monuments, but the churches, basilicas, and other later edifices of the popes, who always had their Roman imperial forebears to draw from in terms of inspiration. Indeed, many of the monuments that tourists come to see while they are in Rome date from the period of the Papal States, which lasted all the way up to the 1870s. Many monuments, like the Castel Sant'Angelo, represent both Roman and Papal architecture, giving Rome and Italy a flavor of the old and new that few countries can match.

Of course, Rome is not the only site in Italy that tourists are anxious to see. Travelers from all over the world are just as anxious to see Florence, with its galleries of Renaissance and late Medieval art, and the other fantastic towns of Tuscany. Tuscany is, indeed, one of the more interesting areas of Italy. It was interesting even to the ancient Romans as it was the home of the Etruscan civilization, which had notable differences from the Roman civilization and predated it. The sites of Florence and Tuscany are just as numerous as Rome, and it is important for travelers to plan ahead so that they do not regret missing anything later.

Milan is a city that some tourists to Italy specifically seek out while others never manage to fit it into their Italian itinerary. Synonymous in Europe with fashion, Milan has other attractions that draw tourists from Europe and all over the world here. There are Milan Cathedral and various other sites in the city of Milan itself, but there is also the region of Lombardy, where travelers are enchanted by Lake Como, Lake Garda, and the charming small towns that dot the Northern Italian landscape. Lombardy also includes cities such as Mantua, Cremona, and many others that present the perfect setting for a day trip or weekend excursion.

Venice is a city like no other. Indeed, many travelers come to Italy solely for this town and leave without visiting anywhere else. Such a trip may seem strange to some, but anyone who has visited Venice will understand why such decided excursions happen. Venice is a city of water, with grand palazzos and spacious churches fronting the city's many canals. There is also a certain air to Venice that some associate with romance. As many think of Italy as a place for lovers, a visit to this blessed nation without visiting Venice does seem like a missed opportunity.

Last, but certainly not least is Sicily, practically a country unto itself. A large island located off the toe of Calabria, Italy is simultaneously part of Italy and not part of it. It is distinct historically from the rest of Italy, subject to waves of invasions by Greeks, Carthaginians, Normans, Saracens, and others throughout its long history. This has created a colorful architectural and cultural makeup for this isle, centrally located in the Mediterranean. Although some travelers never make it to Sicily, the island has been a favored spot for artists, intellectuals, and others interested in small-town Italian life.

Of course, small-town Italian life does require some understanding of Italian life, both the cultural aspect and the language. Tourists should come to Italy equipped with some basic understanding of the Italian language as well as traditions that tourists would be loathing to ignore. Italy is a dream for tourists, but as the saying goes, when in Rome, do as the Romans do. Equipped with this and other knowledge of Italy, you will be ready for your Italian adventure. The beaches, Roman temples, medieval churches and castles, Renaissance art, and other sites have welcomed others and they will welcome you, as well. Your journey into Italy begins with a quick and colorful review of Italian history.

Chapter 1: The History of Italy

If Italy did not have such a fascinating history, there wouldn't be very much to see. The long history of the Italian peninsula is not just something for the history books. This history can be seen in the many monuments that attract millions of tourists to Italy every year. Indeed, even if a traveler is not particularly interested in the history of the Italian nation, it is this history that they experience when they see a Roman column or arch, a medieval church with exquisite Romanesque arches and frescoes, or a Tuscan villa with its Renaissance garden. It is the history of Italy that you experience when you come to this country and education on Italian history can help you better understand what you are seeing. This understanding can also help guide your itinerary.

Take Rome as an example. Most readers know Rome as the capital of the Roman Empire, but this city was also the center of the Papal States, home of the pope. In fact, much of the sites of Rome date from this period, even if they may include spolia from the earlier imperial period. It can be said that Rome represents Italy in microcosm. Unlike in other countries, there is an overlap of historical periods in Italy that is felt all over Italy. Churches in Rome often incorporate earlier pagan temples while many basilicas in Sicily are, in truth, repurposed Saracen mosques. The Roman Empire may have fallen in 476, but it never really went away as many of its practical edifices, which no longer had any use in the Christian period, were transformed into other things. Therefore, Italian history is remarkable for different empires, peoples, and religions all seeming to overlap with one another, creating a rich cultural tradition that can easily be seen by the casual visitor to Italy today. Even the Italian people may be said to represent this legacy of all of the Mediterranean peoples that passed through this land. Perhaps, nowhere is this truer than in Southern Italy with its rich cuisine and cultural peculiarity, making this area not only distinct from other parts of Europe but even from other regions of Italy.

Even the Romans found Italy perplexing. Italy was home to dozens of people in ancient times, of which the Romans were just one of many. Fortunately for the Romans, the strategic location of their city on the Tiber River and the advancements in technology that made these people master builders in the ancient world allowed the Romans to unite all of Italy, and later the entire Mediterranean region. As an example of the complex patchwork of Italy in ancient times, the Romans were surrounded by non-Roman groups such as the Etruscans, Sabines, Sabines, Apulians, Lucanians, Ligurians, Umbrians, Picentines, Greeks, and others. Even in the Roman-controlled region of Latium, known as Lazio in Modern Italian, there were groups that spoke languages other than Latin originally and whom the Romans regarded as distinct from themselves. The Ancient Romans were very conscious of how they were different from others, but this Roman prejudice did not prevent them from forming an empire. Indeed, the Roman policy was one of bringing non-Roman groups into the Roman nation, gradually allowing them to benefit from the privileges of Roman citizenship. Even the great patrician gens Julia, to which Julius Caesar and Augustus belonged, technically originated outside of Rome, in the town of Alba Longa where it is said that they were kings. This process of bringing the best and brightest from fringe areas into the Roman orbit allowed the Roman state to survive in the complex Mediterranean region for over a thousand years.

But Rome is only one story in the book of Italian history, albeit an important one. The story of Italy alone is one of Greeks' "barbarian" invaders like the Gauls, Goths, and Huns, and of the Catholic Church, who became the predominant force in Italian life after the Romans and perhaps may be said to still be the dominant force today. Italian history is the record of the movement of all of these peoples, just as Italian-ness is too an extension of all that has passed through this land.

The Founding of Rome

Historians of Italy tend to spend a lot of time in the early years as it is this period that fascinates the historian. This fascination stems as much from what is not known as it stems from what is known. Like other regions of the Mediterranean region, Italy was inhabited in the Neolithic period as attested by the bones of Neanderthals and other hominids, and by cave paintings. It is not known who the first inhabitants of Italy were in the earliest period of recorded history, which is, between 2000 BCE and 1000 BCE, but they were perhaps the Sea Peoples, or Pelasgians, who settled in many other regions of the Mediterranean.

Historians remain puzzled by the Sea Peoples, who were mentioned both in Classical writings and in historical documents of this early period. The Sea Peoples most likely lived in Italy, Greece, and Turkey. In fact, the Sea Peoples in Italy may have originated in Turkey where they may or may not have been identical or related to the Hittites, a people who successfully defeated the Egyptians. Historians even in the Greek period believed that these Sea Peoples may have been partial ancestors of the Greeks, or at least some of the Greeks, as Greece too were a land where several groups left their mark, although not perhaps as dramatically or in such great numbers as Italy.

Even the Romans did not know where the varied people of Italy in their time came from. Some peoples in the north of Italy were regarded by the Romans as newcomers, that is, arriving on the peninsula later than themselves, but any records that the Romans may have kept on this people or that have long been lost to history. Indeed, as the people of Italy became rapidly Romanized in the Late Republic and early Roman Empire, even the languages of Italy began to disappear.

Before the Romans, there were the Etruscans who have their name to the region now known as Tuscany. The relationship between Rome and the Etruscans has always been the subject of controversy. Rome had Etruscan kings and some believe that the Romans may have been descended from the Etruscans, although the Romans themselves believed that they were descended from the Trojan Prince, Aeneas. This is an interesting historical coincidence as many modern historians believe that the Etruscans most likely originated in Asia Minor (where Troy was located), occupied by the modern nation of Turkey.

Etruscans are perhaps one of the most fascinating ancient peoples to study because of their distinct traditions and especially for their language, which was totally unrelated to any major language in the region. It has been supposed, again, that the Etruscans may have been part of the larger group of Sea Peoples and that theirs was the only language of these peoples to survive in its original form into the historical period. Some scholars in Eastern Europe believe that South Slavic groups may also be descended in part from the Sea Peoples because of alleged similarities between the Etruscan language and Serbo-Croatian.

Wherever the Etruscans came from, they were one of the two primary influencers on the Romans. The other group, of course, was the Greeks. Although most Roman gods were of Greek origin, as was much of Roman art and literature, the oldest aspects of Roman culture was clearly of Etruscan origin, such as the faceless gods called the Lares, and the custom of men and women eating together, reclining on couches. As important as the mysterious Etruscans were to the Romans, there were some aspects of Rome that appear distinctly Roman: originating from no other people. This includes the Latin language, ancestor of many languages in Europe, including French, Spanish, Italian, and Romanian, and architectural features like the arch and the dome.

It is interesting about Rome that it managed to be a distinct civilization that inspired many others while itself clearly being influenced by the Etruscans to the north of Rome and the Greeks to the south. In fact, this may have been the deciding factor that led Rome to rise above the muck of all the petty city-states and tribes in Italy to become one of the most important civilizations in history. Rome's position between these two groups and near the sea allowed it to take the best of its neighbors and to create a civilization uniquely Roman. Indeed, Rome does give the impression of Greece on steroids, an analogy that the Romans probably would have enjoyed. In reality, though, Rome resembled Greece superficially. Culturally, Rome was something different. Just as they were master masonry builders, so too would they be empire builders, drawing inspiration from the Greeks, but accomplishing feats that might have been somewhat more difficult for their forebears.

The Roman Empire
Most nations of Europe and the West owe something to the Romans, whether it is the language, architecture, or aspects of the law. Indeed, a trip to Washington D.C. is like an introduction to Roman architecture. The Roman legacy permeates all aspects of Western life, and in no place is the Roman presence more strongly felt than in Rome itself. To many, Rome is the Eternal City. One of the oldest continually inhabited cities in the world, Rome has been sacked numerous times, as recently as the 16th century, and yet she always rebuilt herself with new monuments often built on the foundation of the old ones.

The earliest inhabitants of Rome, and probably of Italy, where people who have been invariably described as Pelasgians, Cyclopeans, or Etruscans. These are also called the Sea Peoples (referenced earlier) and it is not clear whether the aforementioned groups were all distinct or the same people. What is known as that whoever the early people were; they were eventually supplanted by the Romans themselves. The Romans dated the founding of their city to the year 739 BCE. The city was founded by the brothers Romulus and Remus, who were suckled on the Palatine Hill by a wolf.

The earliest rulers of Rome were seven kings, whom the Roman admitted were of Etruscan origin. The Romans overthrew their kings at about the time that the Greeks were beginning to have problems with the Persians. The Romans replaced their monarchical form with an oligarchy. The democracy that Rome is associated with did not develop until later if it ever actually existed. Indeed, the Roman Senate always maintained an element of aristocratic character, with its patrician families like the Julius Causerie who had a right to sit in the August body as long as they could meet the property requirement.

The character of Roman civilization changed as the Roman Empire grew and the people of the city had to meet new challenges. The fact that the Romans managed to turn their beginnings as a small-city state into an empire is fascinating, and a traveler can see the works that the Romans left as a testament to their greatness. Indeed, even pre-Roman remains have been found in Lazio and the tourist can see these too if interested.

Some historians see the engineering accomplishments of the Romans as the greatest evidence for why their civilization was so successful, but one must also keep in mind the Roman ability to assimilate its neighbors, even the people that invaded Rome throughout its history. Indeed, Rome was frequently invaded by the Celtic Gauls and the Roman people lived in fear of a Celtic invasion until many of the Gauls settled in a region of Asia Minor that became known as Galatia (these people would be the Galatians of the New Testament about 200 years later).

The story of the Romans from the fourth century through to the second century is one of the accidental empires. After the Romans had overcome their immediate neighbors to dominate Central and Southern Italy, Rome found itself becoming involved in wider Mediterranean affairs, such as three major wars against Mediterranean superpower Carthage, and involvement in the internal affairs of the other powers in the region namely the Ptolemies in Egypt and the Macedonian kings on the Greek mainland.

Although some date the founding of the Roman Empire to the assumption of wide powers by Augustus in 27 BCE, the imperial state of Rome actually predates the formation of the military dictatorship. Rome fought three wars with Carthage, finally destroying this city in 146 BCE and annexing its lands. Soon afterward, the Kingdom of Pergamum was left to the Romans by its last king. Rome had already annexed Macedonia and most of Greece at this point. In the next 60 years, Rome would gain a foothold in Syria and the Western regions of North Africa. Perhaps most importantly, Rome managed to finally quell its allies/subordinates on the Italian peninsula in the Social War, which would eventually result in all of the citizens of Italy receiving Italian citizenship and adopting Latin as their language. They had originally spoken dozens of languages, most of which were unrelated to Latin.

The end of the Social War saw Rome stabilized enough to begin to seriously devote itself to an empire. Indeed, at this point, Rome had been transformed from a city-state that had expanded purely in order to survive into an empire that desired to be one. Roman tax collectors and merchants received tangible benefits from the empire and the populist leaders of Rome were happy to oblige them by inventing pretexts to invade foreign lands.

It was at this point that Rome began to change. Its culture became more commercial and materialistic, and the influences from Greece and Egypt (and the Eastern Mediterranean in general) became more palpable. Roman conservatism, dominated by the idea of the paterfamilias who had the right of life and death over his family, began to be supplanted by a sort of cosmopolitanism, in which the Roman senatorial class held on to their sense of Roman-ness, but began to adopt features of the many other peoples that they interacted with, especially in the realm of religion.

At this juncture, the Roman Republic began to fall apart. There were many reasons for this, but it was at least in part due to the wealth that began to flood Rome for overseas, power struggles between plebeians and patricians for control of Rome, and yet other struggles between Romans and Italians, and generals. Indeed, this was the populist period in Rome in which generals exploited the changes in Roman society to fight for prominence. Rome had long been ruled by a curious but stable system by which two executives, known as consuls, served simultaneously. This type of system was not unprecedented in the region as the Spartans also had a system of twin rulers (two kings rather than consuls).

The constant war that Rome dealt with in the first century BCE and the need for stable leadership saw the system of two consuls elected yearly eroded. Indeed, a man hailing from a small town of Latium (i.e. outside of Rome), a man called Gaius Marius, went on to hold the consulship a record seven times as the Romans needed his incomparable military skills to repel invasions by the Cimbri and Teutones (Germanic tribes) and to win a war against the Numidians of North Africa. History is filled with coincidences, or what we may think of as coincidences. Gaius Marius was the uncle of Gaius Julius Caesar, who therefore was able to use this important connection to escape beginnings as an obscure patrician to become perhaps the most famous Roman.

Gaius Marius's time was notable for the Social War and the beginnings of internal, Roman civil wars. The dictatorial example of Gaius Marius would inspire other would-be Roman autocrats, like Lucius Cornelius Sulla, Pompey, and Julius Caesar himself, men who would have been conscious that the Roman Republic was collapsing. Julius Caesar never achieved his supposed dream of becoming King of Rome, even though he had done what many Romans before him had failed to do, overcome the Gauls in what is now France. The feat of restoring the monarchy to Rome would be left to Julius Caesar's great-nephew and adopted heir, Gaius Julius Caesar Octavianus, better known to history as Octavian or Augustus, the name he assumed when he became imperator (emperor).

Augustus brought more than 40 years of stability to Rome. He conquered Egypt, uniting the entire Mediterranean rule for the first, and only, time in history. A decided conservative, Augustus attempted to restore some of the Roman-ness to Rome. The Roman Senate continued to meet, even though all power was now in his hands, and he attempted to restore a semblance of traditional Roman values. Augustus was still a politician, so he knew that Rome needed something to hold it together, as most of its inhabitants were technically neither Romans nor Roman citizens. He created the cult of Augustus and Livia (his wife), allowing non-Romans to invest in the Roman idea through the worship of the emperor and his wife. They still kept their native gods, an example of how the Romans were much less overbearing as overloads compared to other empire-builders.

Rome would experience a period of growth and decline over the next two centuries. The reigns of Nero and Domitian are regarded by historians as low points, while the reigns of Claudius and Trajan tend to be viewed as high points. The death of Marcus Aurelius in the second century saw the beginning of the final decline of Rome. At this stage, Rome had lost its first dynasties and the imperial dignity could fall into the hands of anyone who had the support of the army or had enough denarii to purchase the throne.

By this time, Rome and Italy were well under the influence of what would be its second great influence (after the Roman Empire itself): Christianity. The Roman government continued to persecute Christians right up until the fourth century when Rome would have its first Christian emperor. Before this, Roman emperors had attempted various tactics to attempt to salvage the declining empire, such as war with the rising Parthians in the East, and the granting of citizenship to every free citizen in the empire by Caracalla in the 3rd century.

Constantine the Great would finally end paganism and apostasy in Rome, establishing Christianity as the central religion. In spite of this, the reign of Constantine the Great might be considered as the end of Rome and Italy as power centers in the Mediterranean. Constantine moved his capital to the Greek city of Byzantium, which he renamed Constantinople, and he began to entrench power in the Eastern Mediterranean rather than the West. Although the rise of enemies in this region made this move a necessity, it would mean that the Eastern areas of Rome were protected while Rome and Italy were not.

The Barbarian Invasions and the Early Church
The division of the Roman Empire into eastern and western parts spelled the end of Italy. Emperors reigning in the West would have to deal with enemies who were filled with a vitality that Rome had lost, and who were able to field large armies, which Rome also found itself increasingly unable to do. After invasions by the Huns, Vandals, Goths, and other tribes, much of the Roman Empire was overrun, namely what is now France, Western Germany, and Northern Italy. Italy itself would cease to be under Roman rule with the demise of the last truly Roman emperor, Romulus Augustulus in 476 CE.

Although history does not always make this clear, most of the German barbarians who invaded and overran Rome were admirers of Roman civilization. Perhaps this is why so many monuments of Rome remain today, and even languages descended from Latin continue to exist, even though the lands where they were spoken were almost completely overrun and pillaged, including Italy itself. The Goths established a line of kings who ruled for about 100 years after the fall of Rome. By this time there were popes, who were subordinate to the government in Constantinople until the 9th century. The Eastern Roman or Byzantine emperors managed to regain control of parts of Italy after the Gothic conquest until finally pushed out of the region by the Arabs in the 7th century. At this point, Italy truly entered a Dark Age. This period transformed much of Italy in several significant ways. Germanic groups, like the Lombards who may have originated in Sweden, completely overran Northern Italy, replacing some of the original inhabitants or pushing them southward. Indeed, much of the cultural division between Northern and Southern Italy has to do with the reality of foreign conquest in the North. Regions like Tuscany, Lazio, Umbria, Southern Italy, and Sicily would retain their Roman-era populations although they too were subject to practically ceaseless invasions, the enslavement of their populations, and constant power transfers. Indeed, by the time of the Renaissance, Italy was the most divided state in Europe, with the Aragonese in power in the South, the French invading the North, the Papal States in the center, and dozens of petty rulers and condottieri in other places.

It is this divided time in Italy that gave rise to much of the regional differences in language, cuisine, and culture that characterizes Italy today. Indeed, many travelers to Italy are unaware of the great variety that characterizes this nation of about 60 million people. An interesting case to examine is that of Sicily, which was invaded by the Arabs in the 7th century, reconquered by the Byzantines, conquered again by the Arabs, and then conquered by the Normans from France around the time of the Crusades. This means that the Sicilian people have elements of pre-Roman, Roman, Greek, Arab, North African, and Norman French (Germanic) genetics and culture, all the while speaking a language that is, along with Sardinian, among the most divergent in Italy. Indeed, the famous Italian actress Claudia Cardinale spoke in Sicilian in her starring roles and had to be dubbed in Italian, as she could not speak the language.

The Renaissance and Later

It is the Renaissance that many think of when they dream of Italy. This period which lasted for over 100 years gave rise to one of the most creative artistic and scientific movements in recorded history. This movement is even more remarkable in that it is superimposed on all the historical periods and cultures that predated it. So you can see Renaissance frescoes and paintings in Roman buildings converted into churches. You find Renaissance gardens built on top of known gardens of the late Roman Republic. You find Renaissance busts and sculpture in the style of earlier Greek and Roman portraiture, et cetera.

What is even more curious about the Renaissance is that it began in a region as fervently Catholic as Central Italy. Central Italy was the power base of the popes. These popes were elected by the College of Cardinals, as they still are today, and were ecclesiastical rulers in name only. Indeed, they had secular power just as great as any king and they sometimes led their Papal armies into war personally, dressed in plate armor. The popes were among the primary commissioners of the art of the Renaissance, creating works that were superficially religions, but in fact inventive and almost transgressive works of art if one reads between the lines.

The Renaissance period, even if characterized by the calamitous invasion of Rome in 1526, would return Italy to its central position in Europe, a position it had not held in 1000 years. Indeed, the sort of art that was being produced in Italy at this time had not been seen since the period of ancient Rome. But this wasn't just a time of art. The period was also notable for the scientific discoveries, and rediscoveries, and cultural explosion that set Europe on a path to become known for what it is today: a center of European culture.

The Renaissance was also a time of confusion. It was the time of the condotierri, the warlords who battled for control of northern and central Italy. In fact, this was the end of the condotierri as power bases began to emerge in Italy, namely the French in the north, the popes in the center, and the Spanish in the south. The Aragonese who had controlled Naples and Sicily in the Late Middle Ages was succeeded by the Spanish monarchy of the Habsburgs and later the Bourbons. There would still be petty states in Northern Italy, some of them descended from condotierri rulers and others descended from the illegitimate children of popes and other Roman noblemen, but they would fall under the sway of the Bourbons and later the Habsburgs until these petty dynasts were gradually replaced in the years leading up to the French Revolution.

The Medici was, of course, among the more important of these regional powers. They had begun as Florentine bankers in the Middle Ages and rose to prominence, intermarrying with some of the most important dynasties in Europe, like the Habsburgs and Valois, and gaining control over all of Tuscany, which they ruled until the main branch of the dynasty became extinct in the 18th century. Another important regional power was the Venetians, who brought a measure of stability to the Mediterranean Sea (for economic purposes) even if it meant that other states were forced into the Venetian orbit.

Venice would view with Rome in the Early Modern period for cultural prominence in Italy. The republic was the home of men like Titian, Canaletto, and Tiepolo, who established a reputation for Venetian art, which allowed Venice to maintain an independent cultural identity right up until the conquest of the city by the French after the French Revolution. Although small states like Venice and Mantua lost their independence in these later years, Italy would continue to be divided right up until the 19th century, even if the southern regions became united in the restored Kingdom of the Two Sicilies after the defeat of Napoleon.

The unexpected power in the region would be the House of Savoy in the Kingdom of Savoy. Ruling the regions of Savoy and Piedmont along the French border as well as the island of Sardinia, the House of Savoy would prove to be the only dynasty with enough stability and vitality to unite Italy, even if this dynasty was not particularly remarkable by European standards. The Sardinians would wage war against the two main powers in Italy – the Austrians who ruled Lombardy and Veneto in the north, and the Popes who still controlled Central Italy. They would join with Italian nationalists in the South to unite most of Italy in the Kingdom of Italy in 1861. With the formation of this state, Italy became unified for the first time since the fall of the Romans in 476. Italy began to experience somewhat of cultural fusion, though regional differences in culture in Italy still persist to the present. Italy would go through periods of imperialism and fascism as it sought to create an identity for itself in the modern world. Millions of Italians would leave their homeland in this time of industrial and cultural change for places like the United States, Argentina, Brazil, and many other lands where their descendants brought with them the memory of Italy.

Quick Review of Italian Geography

A quick review of Italian geography will be of benefit to the reader planning a trip to the country. Italy is a member of the European Union and NATO, and it is neighbored by France, Switzerland, Austria, and Slovenia. Italy also includes two smaller nations: Vatican City and San Marino. Many tourists to Rome incorporate the Vatican into their travels. Travelers to Umbria and the Marche can also swing by San Marino, although this may take some dedication on the part of the tourist.

Italy's geography gives it a warmer climate than most other nations in Europe. This is both because it is more southerly than most European countries, but also because it is surrounded by the sea in the extreme north. Italy is a land of great geographic diversity, with mountains, hills, and fertile valleys scattered all across the land. Although there is much fertile land in Italy, there are several regions dominated by mountains, especially in the interior and north of Italy.

Italy is a long, narrow country that juts out into the Mediterranean Sea. A quick look at a map reveals that Italy is shaped like a boot. The region of Apulia is the heel of the boot while Calabria is the toe. Off the coast of Calabria is the island of Sicily, a large island with a long history. The other major Italian island is the more mysterious Sardinia, which is located northwest of Sicily, south of the French region of Corsica (inhabited by people of Italian origin).

Italy, a nation of approximately 60 million people, is divided into regions and provinces. The regions represent historical areas of Italy and these are broken down into provinces, which are generally named after their capital city. For example, the Province of Milan lies in the Region of Lombardy. The regions of Italy are listed below:

- Lazio
- Marche
- Tuscany
- Umbria
- Emilia-Romagna

- Friuli-Venezia Giulia
- Trentino-Alto Adige/Sudtirol
- Veneto
- Aosta Valley
- Liguria
- Lombardy
- Piedmont
- Abruzzo
- Apulia
- Basilicata
- Calabria
- Campania
- Molise
- Sardinia
- Sicily

Chapter 2: How to Plan a Trip to Italy

The first step in your Italian vacation will be planning your trip. Although many travelers, especially from neighboring European countries, may choose to visit Italy without much prior planning, travelers planning a longer stay or coming from overseas, like the United States or Canada, may want to put some thought into planning their trip. Planning your trip will consist of thinking about such questions as:

- Where in Italy you would like to visit
- How long you plan to stay in Italy
- Whether to focus on one region of Italy or visit several
- Whether to incorporate beaches into your visit
- When to visit

Answering these questions will help you figure out both where the best place in Italy to visit for you is and when might be a good time to visit. Although in this book we focus on the more popular regions of Italy for tourists, travelers should keep in mind that all regions of Italy receive tourists in sizeable numbers, so you can easily choose to forego Rome and focus on Sardinia or Piedmont instead. Your Italian vacation is just that, your vacation, and there is no wrong decision in terms of where to visit.

Working with a Travel Agent or Planning a Trip on Your Own
Perhaps the first question to answer is whether to work with a travel agent or to plan a trip on your own. Advantages of working with a travel agent include being able to be part of a tour group (which some overseas tourists prefer) and getting package deals on hotels, airfare, and even restaurants. Although travel agents are capable of scheduling many different types of trips, they are especially good at package trips to certain regions of Italy, like Sicily, Tuscany, or Rome, and they can be a good choice for people who plan on a more focused trip.

For those travelers planning a more exhaustive or non-traditional tour of Italy, you may want to think about putting your travel itinerary together yourself. For example, some travelers may want to visit Rome and Venice all in one trip. Or perhaps they were planning on focusing on Sicily, but they also want to see Genoa and the beaches of Sardinia. A dedicated travel agent can help you set up this type of trip, but you may also consider planning such a trip on your own.

The aspects of planning a vacation on your own are just the sorts of things you would expect. You will have to book flights to and from Italy, as well as flights to and from different regions of Italy if they are very different. Keep in mind that some islands of Italy may only be reachable by ferry, such as Elba, the Aeolian Island, et cetera. One advantage of using a travel agent if you plan to visit more obscure sites is that they can help you if you run into problems, such as needing to reschedule dates or changing routes. Because of language differences, this can be more difficult to do in Italy if you are not working with a travel agent, although it is certainly not impossible.

Of course, planning a trip on your own allows you to be the complete master of your itinerary. Planning a trip this way would have been more difficult twenty or thirty years ago, but it certainly is possible in this day and age of the internet and travel apps. Hotels and flights can easily be booked online, you will just have to keep in mind things like how far apart sites and cities are and whether your travel plans are reasonable based on distances in Italy. Also, make sure that you do not spend all of your funds on travel and accommodation. You will also need funds set aside for taxicabs, restaurants, tip, souvenirs, and the like.

Best Times to Visit Italy

There really is no such thing as the best time to visit Italy. Because Italy does have many beaches that tourists often desire to visit, many people choose to come in the summertime, although this tends to be a busier time for obvious reasons. Travelers should make sure to plan summer travel to Italy months in advance. Hotels may be booked if this is not handled ahead of time. Even beaches may be booked in summer months. Some sites in Italy may be visited in the fall or spring, especially if you do not plan on spending a lot of time on the beach. Even beaches can be visited at these times because of the Italian climate. It may be advisable for the tourist looking to get the most out of Italy to avoid the dead of summer, July and August for example, but everyone's needs are different.

Getting around Italy
Sites in Italy can be reached by plane or by air. The largest airline in Italy is Alitalia, although most European and American carriers fly to airports in Italy. The two largest airports in Italy by passenger numbers are in Rome (Fiumicino) and Milan (Malpensa). Italy has an active rail network, including high-speed trains that run between Milan and Naples. Italy also has great roads that are state-owned but privately run, if you plan on renting a car.

Best Places to Visit in Italy
It is not easy to narrow down the best places in Italy for tourists to see because there are so many. Sites on the itineraries of many travelers include the Grand Canal in Venice, the Colosseum in Rome, the museums of Florence, and the Leaning Tower of Pisa in Pisa, Tuscany. Because there is so much to see, we narrowed down our list of top sites to five cities and regions. You can begin your travels there. We also touch on other sites in our list of the best Italian beaches. The following chapters will cover the following five areas:
- Rome

- Florence and Tuscany
- Venice
- Milan and Lombardy
- Sicily

Chapter 3: Rome

Many travelers to Italy come to Rome. There is an allure to Rome that is only matched by a handful of places in the world, including cities like Paris and Venice that has also a similar sort of mythos that has grown over the ages. But there is no place in the world like Rome. Rome was long the greatest city in the world, a city that Julius Caesar found brick and left marble. It is amazing to think that the monuments of that distant past can still be seen and experienced today, allowing modern people to breathe the same air that the great men of the past breathed.

But Rome is more than just a city of ruins. As the capital of Italy, Rome is still a city of people: residents who are well aware of how fortunate they are to live in this place. Rome is also home to the Vatican, the center of the popes for nearly two thousand years. Indeed, Rome only became the capital of Italy in 1870, after an agreement between the king of Italy and the Papal government saw almost the entirety of the remaining Papal State annexed to the kingdom. The pope was relegated to the splendid treasures of the Vatican, a fate that the pontiffs have perhaps become more used to over the years. These many facets of Rome can be seen today. An introduction to Rome, of course, includes the Roman Empire, but as we have seen in our historical review of Italy, the Roman story also includes the popes, the condotierri, the Borgias, the ancient nobility of Rome, and the many common people who over thousands of years gave Rome its character. Indeed, it is fascinating to imagine that the Roman common people of today are descended from the same folk that formed the foundation of the Roman Empire.

Experiencing life among these people is reason enough to visit Rome, although the many sites of Rome are certainly an added bonus. Indeed, Rome is really a city that gives an air of the past more so than of the present. Rome is a city of palazzo with large gardens and grand buildings and hotels at the end of narrow streets. There are many parks, most of which were once private, and there are of course the ruins of the Roman Imperial and Middle Age periods, nestled between buildings that have been requisitioned for a modern purpose.

A trip through Rome, therefore, is not quite the same as a trip to London, New York, or even Paris. You should come to Rome equipped with a map to help you get from one sight to the next, but you should be prepared to perhaps spend hours in the Borghese Gardens or on the Palatine Hill, merely enjoying the uniqueness of the place rather than merely striking another successful accomplishment off of your list. This means that you may want to plan a little more time for Rome. Rome deserves extra consideration and you will not regret it.

Rome was, in ancient times, divided into seven hills. These hills defined the municipal territory of Rome and they still exist to the present, most of them covered with sites of architectural value or present-day buildings. Today, the significance of hills in a city may not seem significant, but to an old school Roman, this would have been an essential part of their daily life, going from one hill to another. The Seven Hills of Rome were:

- Quirinal Hill
- Viminal Hill
- Esquiline Hill
- Caelian Hill
- Capitoline Hill
- Palatine Hill
- Aventine Hill

Sights in Rome can be divided into several categories, all of which will be covered here as we delve into our list of the best places to visit in Rome. There are, of course, ancient sites like the Colosseum and the Baths of Caracalla, but there are also repurposed sites like the Pantheon, religious sites like the Vatican, and secular sites like the Villa Borghese and the Borghese gardens. There are, of course, hundreds of sites in Rome to visit, and you may want to make your own list of unusual sites that appeal to you. Here, we will review the main sites, but it is also important not to neglect some of the more obscure churches and palazzos that might tickle your fantasy.

So what are the top sites in Rome that tourists should visit? These are the sites that no visit in Rome would complete without hitting, but, again, you should always leave some time for less popular sites that may be more memorable for you. Here are the top sites in Rome:

- The Palatine Hill
- The Baths of Caracalla
- The Catacombs
- The Basilica of St. John Lateran (San Giovani in Laterano)
- The Spanish Steps
- The Pantheon
- The Borghese Gallery
- The Roman Forum
- The Vatican
- Colosseum

These sites will be reviewed individually, giving you a sense of what makes each site special. Most likely, you are planning to visit Rome in addition to other places in Italy. Rome is centrally located, so travelers often incorporate Rome into itineraries that focus on Northern or Southern Italy. Therefore, you can add Rome to your Florence, Milan, Venice itinerary, or you can add it to your Naples, Sicily, Sardinian beach itinerary. It is up to you how you choose to work Rome into your travelers. Perhaps you will decide to give up going home altogether and settle permanently in Italy.

The Palatine Hill

The Palatine Hill was the center of the Roman aristocracy during the Roman Republic and the Roman Empire after the Republic fell. This means that the Palatine Hill is filled with hundreds of sites, some of which have yet to be excavated as much of the construction on the Palatine Hill was done on top of previous construction. Therefore, the Roman emperors constructed their enormous palaces on the sites of the aristocratic homes of families like the Julii, Claudii, Domitii, Livii, and others who helped shape the Roman Republic. In fact, the Palatine Hill was so synonymous with palatial homes that our word for palace in English comes from Palatine (see also palazzo in Italian, palais in French, et cetera).

Your tour to the Palatine Hill will include an exploration of the massive sites located on this stretch of land, including the Domus Augustana, the Temple of Cybele (an Anatolian goddess), and the massive arches of the retaining wall, which allowed the emperors to build so grandly on this, one of the original seven hills of Rome.

The Baths of Caracalla

Although Caracalla as an emperor does not have the greatest reputation among the long list of men who ruled Rome, he did leave the city one of the greatest bath complexes the world has ever seen. Bathhouses in Rome were not just a necessity, designed to allow denizens to bathe at a time when space was limited and most people would not have been able to bathe at home, but it was also a place of social exchange, were men met their peers and conversed with them about the goings-on in town. For this reason, the bathhouses were great public monuments, built soaring into the air and covered with multicolored marble and mosaics. A visit to the Baths of Caracalla is one of the best ways to get an understanding of what Rome was. Keep in mind that the ancient Romans built massive aqueducts to carry water to sites like these.

The Catacombs
The Catacombs form an interesting and important part of the Roman legacy. The Catacombs are the subterranean tunnels where the Christians fled during the period of religious persecution in Rome. Although the Romans were, in general, pretty tolerant in terms of religion, they did not accept religions that did not incorporate the imperial cult (that is, of Augustus and other, later, emperors) into their worship. For this reason, Christians were persecuted in Rome right up until the time that the Emperor Constantine the Great became a Christian.

The Basilica of St. John Lateran (San Giovanni in Laterano)

No city in the world is filled with as many churches of artistic and architectural merit as the city of Rome. Some of these churches are converted Roman temples are public buildings, while others were built specifically for the purpose of housing Catholic worship during the more than 1000 years that the popes ruled here. The Basilica of St. John Lateran, known in Italian as San Giovanni in Laterano, is one of the most striking churches in Rome. One of the more important basilica sites in the Papal States, this church is now located in the Italian-controlled City of Rome.

The Spanish Steps

The Spanish Steps, like the Eiffel Tower or the Statue of Liberty, is one of those iconic sites that lovers or anyone interested in a truly authentic experience must see when they visit the city. The irregular steps were not, in fact, built by the Spanish. They take their name from a plaza at the foot of the steps, which is one of many piazzas in Rome, fronted with palaces and sculptures. This area of Rome has more of a baroque quality, and it represents the great variety of architectural styles that can be encountered in Rome.

The Pantheon

The Pantheon was built by the Romans for purposes of worship. Indeed, the word pantheon represented all of the gods in the Greek language, and this edifice was built in the early imperial period and rebuilt in 80 CE after a fire. This building is a monument to Roman architectural skill. It features what was once the largest dome in the world, which supported by a mass of brick and concrete. The interior is also exquisite, so much so that it was later converted into a church. In front of the Pantheon are a 16th-century fountain and an Egyptian obelisk.

The Borghese Gallery

No trip to Rome would be complete without a visit to one of its many museums. Situated in what was once the private property of the Borghese Family, the Borghese Gallery contains art that once belonged to the family. It is situated in a picturesque area of villas and parkland. The gallery is filled with works of art by Renaissance and Baroque artists, including Peter Paul Rubens, Titian, Raphael, and Caravaggio. The gallery is worth visiting for its pleasant surrounds as much for its art, and many Romans consider the gardens here among their favorite sites in Rome.

The Roman Forum
One needs to visit the Roman Forum to really understand Rome. This is not purely because the Forum was filled with grandiose monuments, but because the Forum represented an aspect of Rome that made this state different from others. Rome was, for most of its history, not an autocracy made up of dictator and governed, by democracy or oligarchy comprised of men who understood what it was to be Roman and all worked toward the greatness of Rome. The Forum was the site of important Roman sites like the Curia (Senate House), basilicas (public buildings), temples, and other sites that were important to the Roman people.

The Vatican

The Vatican is home to one of the most important collections of art in the world. Indeed, there is so much art of value in the Vatican, collected over the centuries, that it literally boggles the mind. The Vatican is also home to such important sites as the infamous Sistine Chapel and St. Peter's Square, a site important to Catholics around the world. Besides all that, the Vatican is also home to the pope and the College of Cardinals, who still carries on the day-to-day work of the world's only remaining theocracy. The Pope is not only the head of the Catholic Church, but he is also the ruler of Vatican City, just as he was the ruler of the Papal States before that. Do not forget that the Vatican City, with its picturesque army of Swiss Guards, is an independent country: the home of the Catholic Church. You may want to observe a little more decorum than usual here.

Colosseum
The Colosseum is one of those sites that most tourists to Italy have on their itinerary. Begun by the emperor Vespasian, a member of the Flavian dynasty, the Colosseum was completed by his son Titus who had a brief reign before being succeeded by his brother Domitian. The Colosseum was built in the form of a giant Roman arena, places that were the sites of Roman gladiatorial contests. These contests were not merely places where warriors fought, but they also would have hosted teams of exotic animals, like lions and tigers, who were often set to feed on human beings.
In fact, the Colosseum is unique mostly for its massive size. Otherwise, it resembles in style the Roman amphitheater found throughout the Mediterranean. There are similar arenas in other Italian towns as well as in Spain and France, where the amphitheaters in Arles and Nimes are particularly striking and well-known. A trip to the Colosseum is an experience that travelers will not soon forget.

Chapter 4: Florence and Tuscany

Florence holds a unique place in Italy, quite out of proportion to its size or historical influence. Florence was the home of the Medici family, a clan who began their history as bankers in the Middle Ages – one of several influential Florentine banking families- and who eventually rose to become one of the most important aristocratic families in Europe, providing no less than two queens to France, both of whom were among the most influential in French history. The wealth and prominence of the Medici family are evident in Florence, a town that teems with architectural monuments and art.

Indeed, Florence does seem to be the creation of the Medici family. If it were not for them, then Florence would not be an important city for travelers from around the world to visit. If the Medici had moved their operations to Siena or Arezzo, then we would likely be discussing those cities the same way that we discuss Florence today. But the appeal of Florence has more to it than the beautiful things that the Medici family embellished the city with. Florence lies in the Tuscan region, an area blessed with sunshine, rolling hills, vineyards, and some of the best wines in the world.

Indeed, Tuscany was known for the fruits of its soil even in Roman times, when it was the home of the Etruscans, whom the Romans fought against and later assimilated. Florence is inextricably linked with the Tuscan region, being both the most important city in Tuscany and the beneficiary of all of the great things that Tuscany has to offer. The Medici began their aristocratic journey as rulers of Florence and later became Grand Dukes of Tuscany, a title which they held until the middle of the 18th century when the main branch of the Medici dynasty became extinct in the person of Gian Gastone Medici.

Florence seems to be haunted by the memory of the Medici: by Medici men who murdered their wives and plotted against foreign rulers, all to cement their position in Italy and in the world. The Medici women were no less infamous: Catherine de Medici, queen of France in the 16th century and mother of three French queens, was a patron of Nostradamus and said to be an avid user of poison, keeping poison-makers and alchemists in her employ. This queen was also the mother of Queen Marguerite of Navarre, known in France as Reine Margot, the first wife of King Henry IV of France, the first Bourbon king.

Florence is, therefore, the chain that links Italy to many of the great dynasties and stories of Europe. And the city of Florence is filled with picturesque sites that still retain the memory of the small town that the Medici turned into a great city. Naturally, there are many important sites to see in Florence and in Tuscany. In this chapter, we will review the main sites of the city of Florence, as well as the other cities and regions in Tuscany that are worth visiting while you're here. Tuscany is located in Central Italy, north of Rome, and it can be visited on its own (as many tourists do) or incorporated into tours of Northern Italy or Rome and Southern Italy.

Tuscany is a large region with a lot to see so you may not want to restrict yourself to the eleven sites mentioned here. Feel free to do some research on the region and find sites that may appeal to your own personal tastes. Here are the sites that are must-sees in Florence and Tuscany:

- Duomo (Florence)
- Piazza della Signoria (Florence)
- Uffizi Gallery (Florence)
- Pitti Palace (Florence)
- Ponte Vecchio (Florence)
- Pisa
- Arezzo
- San Gimignano
- Elba
- Siena
- Chianti Wine Region

Duomo (Florence)

The Duomo is the cathedral of Florence. Known in Italian as the Duomo di Firenze, this religious edifice is also known as the Cathedral of Santa Maria del Fiore. This is the church that the Medici devoted themselves to building as a testament not only to the greatness of Florence but to the personal greatness of their family. This church took nearly 200 years to build. Most of the delay was due to the great octagonal dome, which architects seemed unclear on how to complete. The dome was so revolutionary that even though it was completed in 1436, it is still regarded as an important representative of the Renaissance, which was then only just beginning.

Piazza della Signoria (Florence)

The Piazza della Signoria is one of several important squares in Florence. Many Italian cities had a piazza like this, representing the seats of power of the Podesta, or local rulers that ruled many Italian cities during the period of the Germanic Holy Roman Empire. The Piazza della Signoria was the center of the Florentine city-state, and it contained the Palazzo Vecchio (town hall), as well as other important artistic and architectural monuments, including statues by Donatello and Michelangelo. A visit to this plaza makes it clear why Florence and the Medici were so important. How many cities have public squares with art by men the likes of Michelangelo and Donatello? Ahem… we're talking about Renaissance artists here, not ninja turtles.

Uffizi Gallery (Florence)

The greatest cities in Italy are filled with incredible works of art. Indeed, museums in the United States and the United Kingdom vie for the works of art that have rested quietly in Italy for hundreds of years. It is a bit sad that countries like Italy have been denuded of their art by ravenous collectors (who have actually been on the scene for at least 300 years), but collections like the Uffizi prove that Italy still has works in its own country that it can be proud of. Built in a 16th-century office complex (*uffizi* or offices) by Cosimo I de Medici, it was later converted into a place and filled with art. In 2016, it was visited by more than 2 million people.

Pitti Palace (Florence)
The Palazzo Pitti is both a museum and a work of art itself. Indeed, this building has served as inspiration for other important residences, including the home of the Bavarian kings in Munich. This building was one of the main palaces of the Medici monarchy until its demise in the 1700s. It is filled with works of art by the likes of Giorgione, Veronese, Raphael, Caravaggio, Peter Paul Rubens, and Titian. Indeed, the Pitti Palace houses one of the most important Renaissance galleries in the world. Lovers of art would be loath to miss this museum.

Ponte Vecchio (Florence)
The Ponte Vecchio is a fascinating bridge in the Medieval style. This bridge spans the River Arno, which runs through Florence. There were once many bridges in Europe like this, with houses and shops on top of the bridge. The Ponte Vecchio is one of the few that still remain, and the most famous. It is believed that there has been a bridge at this site since Roman times, although the present bridge dates to the 1400s. Although the bridge has been repeatedly damaged by floods, it retains its shops and houses and is likely to remain a popular tourist spot.

Pisa

Pisa is one of the great cities of Tuscany. Indeed, the city of Pisa is a testament to the reality that there is more to Tuscany than Florence. Pisa is located west of Florence on the Arno River, just before that waterway empties out in the Ligurian Sea. There are many sites to see in Pisa, not least of which is the Leaning Tower of Pisa, which, of course, was not intended to lean when it was built. The town is also home to the University of Pisa, one of the oldest in Italy.

Arezzo

Arezzo is a truly ancient town, being the modern version of Arretium, a town which the Romans conquered in the 4th century BCE, over 2000 years ago. Before that, the town was one of the capitals of the Etruscan nation, and even today can be found remains attesting to the active trade with foreign nations that Tuscany (then known as Etruria) engaged in. Arezzo is a very pretty town that features a number of churches and palazzo worth visiting. It even has the remains of an amphitheater dating back to Roman times. Of course, one cannot forget the city wall of Arezzo, a testament to the times when Italy was a country at war.

San Gimignano

San Gimignano is one of the iconic sites of Italy. This hill town of medieval towers is a frequent image on postcards, even some dating back to the 19th century. The center of this town has been listed as a UNESCO World Heritage site because of its monuments, including its central square, communal palace, and, of course, its many towers. San Gimignano is even known for its cuisine, including its ham and its saffron. The city has some notable museums, and the environs of the town are picturesque. You may also know San Gimignano for its white wine.

Elba

Elba is an island in the Ligurian Sea that we will encounter later in our discussion of the best beaches in Italy. Indeed, Elba, a relatively small island, is blessed with several beaches that make this isle the perfect setting for a one or two-day excursion. Elba is easily reached by ferry from the Tuscan town of Piombino. Elba was known as a site of iron mining from ancient times, including by the Greeks who called the place Aethalia. Today, Elba is home to several pretty towns, including Portoferraio (referencing iron) and Capoliveri. Come here for the small town feel of Italy and, of course, for the beaches.

Siena

Siena is one of those cities that should be on a complete itinerary of Italy. Unfortunately, Siena often gets missed in favor of more traveled places like Rome, Florence, Venice, and Milan. Siena, with its monuments like its cathedral and Public Square, has much to see. Siena, in particular, is home to festivals that harken back to the Middle Ages when city-states like Siena had their own independent identities and local cultures. Siena was one of the last places in Tuscany to be conquered by Florence, and you can get a sense of the uniqueness of the town by paying a visit. The city is located south of Florence on the way to Rome.

Chianti Wine Region

Tuscany is known for many things. It is known for its great cities like Florence and Pisa. It is known for its picturesque rolling hills with villas, castles, and other sites to delight the traveler. But it is also known for its wine. We mentioned wine in the context of San Gimignano, but Tuscany is also known for the Chianti Wine Region. This area exists in sort of a triangle formed by the cities of Florence, Arezzo, and Siena. This region is home to numerous wineries, not to mention the characteristic Romanesque churches of the region. Because this wine region was fought over by Florence and Siena, it is also home to hilltop castles, themselves a lure for many travelers. Chianti is a wooded region, too, remarkable for its oaks, cypresses, and chestnuts.

Chapter 5: Venice

Venice is one of the unique cities of the world situated on canals at the edge of the Tyrrhenian Sea. Venice was the capital of a large maritime empire that controlled sites throughout the Mediterranean Sea, including in the Greek Islands. Indeed, Venice's wealth came from trade, allowing the small city to maintain its independence right up until the French conquered it in 1797. Like many other Italian cities, Venice's monuments attest to its storied past as an independent city-state, and the wealth that trickled was devoted to the creation of many of the monuments described here.

Venice is located in a region called the Veneto, an area of Northeastern Italy noted for its flat terrain filled with Palladian villas and picturesque towns. Indeed, the Veneto formed a power base for the Venetians, as the residents of this town quickly subjugated their neighbors and established control over their region, which they maintained for hundreds of years. It is important to point out Venice's place in the Veneto, as this makes Venice somewhat distant from other places in Italy (with the exception of Milan in neighboring Lombardy) and it also points out those places that travelers may want to visit while they are in the region.

In terms of a quick geography lesson, Venice lies on a series of islands that are connected by canals, the most important of which is called the Canale Grande, the Grand Canal. The islands of Venice lie in a large lake of sorts, a lagoon, sheltered by a barrier island known as the Lido. Venice's aqueous situation seemed to lend itself to a nation with pretense toward a maritime empire. And this is just what Venice became. Venetian vessels dominated the Mediterranean for nearly six hundred years, creating a powerful state that was both a mercantile republic and an aristocratic oligarchy. A voyage to Venice is like stepping back into a time that no longer exists, which is perhaps why Venice continues to fascinate romantics and academics alike.

Venice can be visited as part of a travel tour just to Venice, or it can be incorporated into itineraries that include Milan and Tuscany. Many people who visit Venice also are interested in visiting towns like Verona, Brescia, Padua, and Vicenza. Fair Verona was, of course, the site of William Shakespeare's Romeo and Juliet, and this town has long been a popular tourist stopover. It is easy to hop over to Verona after a stay in Venice.

Aside from these towns, Venice is also surrounded by palaces and villas built by the Venetian elite. Of course, if one is interested in aristocratic residences, Venice teems with them: a reminder of the families who cemented their power in the form of the office of the doge. While in Venice, make sure to embark on a romantic gondola ride, which may require that you enlist the aid of a paramour to be romantic with (if you do not already have one). Below is a list of some of the sites in Venice that you may like to visit while you are there:

- Lido
- Verona
- Rialto Bridge
- Grand Canal
- Doge's Palace
- St. Mark's Basilica

Lido

The Lido is the barrier island that separates the lagoon on which Venice rests from the Adriatic Sea. Long a region outside the aristocratic sphere, the Lido began to be a tourist resort area in the 19th century, reaching a pinnacle of popularity in the early 20th century. The popularity of the Lido owes much to the new popular pastime of going to the beach, which emerged in the relatively conservative time period of the mid-19th century. Now this fashionable area is home not only to miles of beach, but to hotels, and other sites were travelers are sure to meet likeminded people from other countries and find plenty to do.

Verona

Although technically not in Venice, Verona is near enough to the Veneto's capital to warrant a visit by anyone interested in visiting a smaller town, or in seeing the fictional site of Shakespeare's Romeo and Juliet. The home of the Montagues and Capulets, Verona has sites of its own to attract the visitor, including the Roman amphitheater, the Verona Arena, Porta Borsari, several churches and basilicas, and the Piazza dei Signori.

Rialto Bridge

As a city built on canals, Venice is naturally home to many bridges. One of the most well-known of these is the Rialto Bridge, the oldest of all of the bridges spanning the Grand Canal, the main waterway of Venice. The first bridge here was built in the 1100s, although the present bridge dates to the late 16th century. This bridge with its high arch is a romantic site for couples to visit while in Venice, as well as one of the top tourists' sites in Venice in general.

Grand Canal

The Canale Grande, or Grand Canal, traverses through the center of Venice, making sort of an S-curve. It is about two miles long and is crossed by only four bridges. If you plan on going to Venice, you better get used to boats as much of your excursions in the city will take place on a gondola. The Grand Canal was a center of Venetian life, and an address here was necessary for anyone who desired influence in the city. Of course, those days are long gone and rides on gondola are primarily the preserve of romantically inclined tourists rather than relatives of the doge.

Doge's Palace and Bridge of Sighs

The doge, or duke, was the patrician ruler of Venice. This position was monopolized by the aristocratic families of Venice, who cemented their power by gaining this central executive position. The Doge's Palace, also called the Palazzo Ducale, was the home and worksite of the doge, who maintained Venice's wide interests by keeping up this lavish showplace. There can be a wait to get into this place, but a guided tour can take you through the lines and show you the parts of the palace that are generally closed off. A connected site to see here is the Bridge of Sighs.

St. Mark's Basilica
St. Mark's Basilica is a huge church for such a space-constrained city as Venice. Located on St. Mark's Square, Venice's only major public space, this church is probably the most recognizable site in Venice because of its characteristic domes that look more Middle Eastern than Italian. Indeed, Venice got the ducats to build this church from its often predatory excursions into the Greek lands and the Middle East. Venice profited from the decline of the Byzantine Empire: Venetian merchants easily supplanting their Greek predecessors and drawing that wealth in trade to their home town.

Chapter 6: Milan and Lombardy

Milan is both a unique site in Europe and a characteristic Northern Italian city. The largest city (and heart) of Lombardy, Milan is synonymous with high fashion and top-of-the-line European culture. This is nothing new. During the period of Spanish and Austrian rule, which lasted right up until the Italian Reunification, Milan was a center for culture in the region. Its opera house was famous and it was one of several European cities that vied as important cultural centers in the period leading up to the Revolution.

Indeed, much of Milan's history in the Early Modern period was characterized by foreign rule, but before that Milan was the center of the most important state in Northern Italy: the Duchy of Milan, ruled by the Visconti and Sforza dynasties successively. The Dukes of Milan were technically vassals of the Holy Roman Empire, but they were actually condotierri who ruled a number of important cities of Lombardy with Milan at its center. Because of its location in Northern Italy, Milan was a convenient point of access to both France and the German-speaking lands.

This location allowed Milan to be influenced by the rich culture of the late Middle Ages in France and other neighboring regions. Milan was also the site of a particularly Lombard cultural life, with petty wars, courtly romances, and intrigue. Lombardy was, like most of Northern Italy, swept up into the Guelph and Ghibelline wars of the Middle Ages. Milan, as the most important city in the region, managed to subjugate its neighbors under the Visconti dynasty. There are many churches and other monuments from the Visconti period, and these sites are often recognizable for the biscione symbol of the Visconti house: the image of a giant serpent swallowing a man whole.

Milan fell under the orbit of the Sforza family when a condotierro, Francesco Sforza, conquered Milan in 1450 to become fourth Duke of Milan. This was the period of the Late Middle Ages and Early Renaissance, an age of cultural reawakening, which must have made Milan an interesting place to live at the time. Milan's problem, of course, was its central location in Northern Italy. This meant that Milan was both a great fortress for the Sforza family as well as a target for foreign invasion by the Spanish and French.

Indeed, Milan had been founded by the Romans as Mediolanum, in what was then an area of a Celtic settlement. Mediolanum was in the region of Cisalpine Gaul, which in its early history was regarded as being outside of Italia because it was not inhabited by Italian tribes but by Celts and others. In fact, the Romans founded several cities called Mediolanum, of which modern-day Milan is the most famous. In fact, the towns of Evreux and Saintes in France were also called Mediolanum by the Romans, which may have indicated the center of a Celtic tribal confederation.

Milan reached a high point in the Late Middle Ages under the Sforza dynasty, but this was to be short-lived. The French under Louis XII invaded Italy in the early 16th century, leading to an important stage of the famous Italian Wars that would leave most of Italy under the control of foreign powers for more than two hundred years. The essential cause of the Italian Wars were the various claimants to the throne of the Kingdom of Naples, but because armies had to cross through Northern and Central Italy to reach Naples, these were the areas that were most devastated. Milan was conquered by the French and Rome was sacked by mutinous troops in 1527. This was a dark period for Milan and for Italy, although the centuries that followed would eventually lead to a cultural flowering, albeit under foreign influence.

The sites of Milan are a mix of early Roman sites, medieval sites of the Visconti and Sforza periods, and sites from the period of Habsburg rule through the Baroque and Rococo periods. This means that Milan is just as notable as its Roman arches and medieval churches as it is for its Baroque palaces and gardens. Milan, like other sites in Italy, therefore represents the several distinct periods that Italy passed through in a way that is quite unique in Europe. Countries like France, Spain, and Britain are characterized by periods of smooth transition through times of peace, while in Italy one is met with the ruins of destroyed cities and civilizations and the fortifications of nearly constant warfare.

Like the Phoenix, Milan always managed to rise from the ashes of war in the region. Indeed, Milan is the center of the wealthiest region of Italy, home of the stock exchange of Italy, the A.C. Milan football team, and companies like Alfa Romero and other economic powerhouses. Milan is the economic center of Italy, even if the capital is in Rome, and most foreign companies in Italy have their main office in Milan.

Of course, Milan is also filled with tourist sites, and if you are planning to visit Milan you most likely are doing it to see these rather than for economic reasons. Because there is so much to draw the traveler to Milan, you can easily work other aspects of the high life of Milan into your travels, such as shopping or exploring the castles and vineyards in the region. Because Milan is in the center of the wealthy and beautiful Lombard region, many travelers incorporate visits to neighboring cities into their Milanese trip.

Lombardy is the most populous region of Italy, with over 10 million inhabitants, about one-sixth of the Italian population. There are many cities worth visiting in this region, but some of the more prominent include Pavia, Mantua, Lodi, Cremona, Brescia, Bergamo, and, of course, Como, lying at the foot of the glacial Lake Como. Your trip to Milan and Lombardy can be tailored to your needs, but below is a list of the biggest draws in the region:

- Civica Galleria d'Arte Moderna
- Naviglio Canal
- Cimitero Monumentale
- Sant'Ambrogio
- Pinatoteca di Brera
- La Scala Operahouse
- San Maurizio
- Galleria Vittorio Emanuele II
- Castello Sforzesco
- Santa Maria delle Grazie (and Leonardo's Last Supper)
- Como
- San Salvatore-Santa Julia in Brescia
- Mantua
- Milan Cathedral

All but three of these sites are in the city of Milan itself, with the others being easily accessible by rail or other transportation. Hitting these sites will allow the traveler to take in the more important historical, artistic, and architectural sites in the region, although there is so much to see in Milan that it is difficult for many to hit all of the sites in the time that they have. A traveler who is particularly interested in art can also add to their itinerary the several museums that have not been mentioned here, such as the Museo Bagatti Valsecchi and the Poldi-Pezzoli Museum.

Civica Galleria d'Arte Moderna

Milan's Modern Art Gallery is a must-see for any traveler to Milan. The gallery is housed in the Villa Reale, which is the building where Napoleon lived when he visited Milan. It was built in the late 18th century for the Belgioso noble family. This gallery hosts art from the 18th to the 20th centuries, primarily from prominent French and Italian painters like Manet, Gauguin, and Filippini, although it also includes works from the likes of Vincent Van Gogh. The building also has temporary exhibitions, and the site is also worth visiting for its setting and the architectural merit of its main building.

Naviglio Canal

Canals always draw travelers, especially those with romantic intent in mind. Although the canals of Venice may be more famous, the Naviglio is Milan's entrant into the best Italian canal race. The Naviglio is lined with elegant cafes and music venues, and it is possible for travelers to take boat rides down its still waters. This is a popular site to visit at night, and it can easily be incorporated into a Milan itinerary that includes visiting other sites in the day. In the spring, the environs of the canal teem with flowers and there are several markets that pop-up in the area.

Cimitero Monumentale

The Cimitero Monumentale is both a cemetery, as its name indicates, and an outdoor sculpture gallery. One of the two largest cemeteries in Milan, the Cimitero Monumentale dates from 1866, and since then it has been filled with mausolea in the shape of Greek temples, chapels, obelisks, and works of art. One of the most important things to see here is the Famedio, which is at the entrance. It is the main chapel of the cemetery, and it was made in the Neo-Medieval style, like much of the other buildings here. There is also an Art Nouveau flair to many of the tombs and monuments, which should not come as a surprise considering the time period. Some of the notable people buried here include Alessandro Manzoni and Italian painter Francesco Hayez.

Sant'Ambrogio
Sant'Ambrogio is a massive Milanese church and an important example of Romanesque architecture. It dates from the 1100s, although portions of the church originate from the 9th century and early. Indeed, the first church here was built in 386 by Saint Ambrose, who is the patron saint of the city of Milan. This church is an art historian's dream as it contains examples of art from the Dark Ages when churches were the main sponsors of art in Europe. Be sure to visit the various altars and sarcophagi while you are here.

Pinatoteca di Brera

This building was originally a college of the Jesuits, but it has been an art gallery since the late 18th century. This building also contains an observatory and a library in addition to the gallery. The art here was accumulated in various ways, including from the many churches that were demolished or close in the two centuries since the French Revolution. The gallery contains works of art by Titian, Veronese, Moroni, and Tintoretto, as well as many others. There are also frescoes by Bramante of the Umbrian school. The art does not end here. There is a well-known painting by Raphael that is a must-see, as well as works by Flemish masters Rubens and Van Dyck, and works by El Greco and Modigliani. In the courtyard, travelers will be met by an outstanding sculpture of Napoleon Bonaparte by Canova.

La Scala Operahouse
La Scala is regarded by many as the premier opera house in Europe, a position that it has held since the 18th century. At the time, opera was quite popular in Europe, and La Scala was the site of many premieres by well-known composers like Salieri, Rossini, and Verdi. The opera season here starts in December and lasts through May, but tickets can be very difficult to come by. There is also a theater museum in the opera building, where you can see a collection of important historical costumes.

San Maurizio

San Maurizio is one of several religious sites worth visiting in Milan. Indeed, although tourists often come to Italy for the Roman ruins, the beaches, or the romantic sites of Tuscany and Florence, many of Italy's most outstanding monuments are of the religious variety. There is no shortage of these in Milan. Indeed, Milan and the Lombardy region, in general, contain a number of notable sites from a very early period. San Maurizio is regarded by some as one of the most beautiful churches in Milan because of its interior from the 1500s. This church belonged to a monastery and was built on the site of a Roman circus and portions of the Roman walls of Mediolanum. These are now part of the Civic Archaeology Museum of which the San Maurizio Church is a part.

Galleria Vittorio Emanuele II
The Galleria Vittorio Emanuele is one of the most lavish shopping complexes in the world. Indeed, this gallery was constructed at a time when Italy had just been unified, and there was a desire for great monuments like these to show that Italy was a nation on par with countries like France and Britain. Indeed, is it hard to believe that this lavish building with its glass ceiling was built primary for shopping, although even the Romans were known to put great architectural know-how into their commercial basilicas. This building was erected between 1865 and 1877, and it was the largest shopping arcade on the European continent when it was erected.

Castello Sforzesco

This fortress was the center of government of the Sforzas who ruled Milan from 1450 until the early 16th century. Members of this family still exist, although they lost their political prominence in the Italian Wars. Indeed, even members of the earlier Visconti family still exist, including famous Italian director Lucchino Visconti who was active in the 60s and 70s. The Castello Sforzesco is a massive castle that attests to the need to match military function with civil needs. This was a time of war, and a visit to the Castello Sforzesco is like a pleasant trip back in time.

Santa Maria delle Grazie (and Leonardo's Last Supper)
This Gothic church is worth a visit for several reasons, not the least of which is that it hosts Leonardo da Vinci's Last Supper. This church is built of brick, which is more characteristic of Lombardy and Northern Italy in general than Southern Italy. Although the church was severely damaged in the Second World War, it has been restored, including the art in the dome which had been covered up. Of course, the main draw to the church is the Last Supper, which is painted on a wall. It was done between 1495 and 1497 and is one of the most important works of the Italian Renaissance.

Como

The town of Como lies at the foot of Lake Como, one of several lakes in this Alpine region of Northern Italy. Como has been inhabited since Roman times, and it is one of the several sites that claim to be the birthplace of the poet Catullus. Como is also associated with both Pliny the Elder and Pliny the Younger, as well as with Cosima von Bulow, the second wife of Richard Wagner, who was famously portrayed by Silvana Mangano in the film *Ludwig* by Lombard native son Lucchino Visconti. Como is worth a visit for its beautiful lake, picturesque towns, and the multiple villas that dot the region. It is not hard to incorporate Como into your travels, but make sure to bring your checkbook.

San Salvatore-Santa Giulia in Brescia
Brescia is a town picturesquely situated at the foot of the Alps Mountains in Lombardy. It is filled with a number of important sites, although it is perhaps best known in Italy as being an industrial town. The San Salvatore-Santa Julia complex in Brescia was inscribed as a UNESCO World Heritage site because of its monastic buildings from the period of Lombard kings (approx. 8th century), as well as the remains of Roman buildings, such as a Roman theater and forum. In Roman times, this town was known as Brixia.

Mantua

Mantua is a Lombard town that is closely associated with the art of the Late Middle Ages and early Renaissance period. This town was surrounded on three sides by water, which was helpful in protecting it from the frequent invasions that characterized life in Northern Italy, but which also may have given it somewhat of an unhealthy climate. The Mantua of today, however, is a pretty town filled with the monuments of the Gonzago family, who went from being local Podesta to Duke of Mantua, until their line failed in the 18th century. Here, travelers can see the historic old town, a UNESCO World Heritage Site, as well as numerous churches and palazzo museums.

Milan Cathedral

Il Duomo is perhaps the site that visitors are most interested in seeing when they come to Milan, which is why we saved it for last. The Milan Cathedral, known in Italian as Il Duomo, was built over a period of 600 years. The Cathedral was begun in 1386, during the medieval period, and was not completed until the 1960s. It was begun by the then archbishop of Milan and is still the center of the archiepiscopate of Milan. At the time it has begun, the city was ruled by the Visconti, who was anxious to create a monument to their power in their capital. Il Duomo is perhaps best known for its elaborate façade with its many small spires. The desire to finish the façade of the cathedral was actually the work of Napoleon who was anxious to be crowned King of Italy here. Napoleon was crowned here, although it appears that the first façade was not completed until decades later. The remaining details of the exterior were not completed until 1965, and the cathedral has recently been the site of renovation work in the 21st century.

Milan Cathedral is worth visiting for its fantastic façade, its sculptures and stained glass windows, its vast interior, and for the works of art scattered about the historically important space. It is also possible for tourists to walk on the rough. The cathedral contains several chapels with important tombs, reliquaries, and works of art. Near the entrance of the cathedral, tourists can actually descend below the cathedral square to see the remains of early Christian monuments (4th century).

Chapter 7: Sicily

Sicily represents Italy in dramatic fashion. As Italy represents frequent periods of invasion and the passage of many different peoples through the territory, Sicily represents a perhaps more dramatic example of this, positioned as it is at the southernmost point of Italy. This triangular island was inhabited by humans from a very early period and it has the monuments to attest to that. The first major civilization to establish a presence here was that of the Greeks, who established multiple cities here, of which the most famous was perhaps Syracuse, located on the eastern coast of the island.

Indeed, in the fourth century BCE, Syracuse became the largest and wealthiest city in the Greek world, taking over from the cities of mainland Greece, which were embroiled in a state of nearly constant warfare. Syracuse managed to subjugate some of the neighboring Greek towns of Sicily and Southern Italy but declined as the Romans began to rise in power beginning in about the 3rd century BCE. In fact, Syracuse was experiencing its own problems in the form of civil wars and invasions by foreign powers, like the Carthaginians.

The Greek period in Sicily is notable for its monuments, especially the temples at Agrigento and Selinunte. Indeed, Sicily and Southern Italy contain the most important Greek monuments in Italy. In fact, these regions contain some of the largest Greek temple ruins in the entire world. The Greek political power on the island was replaced by that of the Romans who successfully managed to quell Carthaginian influence. Many readers will be familiar with the famous Carthaginian general Hannibal, who was defeated by the Romans in the 2nd century BCE. Sicily, as a Roman province, became notable as an important source of grain to the growing city of Rome in the early years of the Roman Empire.

Indeed, Sicily was an important possession for the Romans. In fact, Sicily was coveted by most of the empires that rose and fell in the Mediterranean region. The Romans managed to bring a measure of stability here, but with the fall of the Roman Empire in the 5th century, Sicily found itself a frequent target for invasions. Perilously located near the North African coast, Sicily was fought over by the Arab caliphates as well as by the Byzantines, who were anxious to regain a measure of Roman control over the wealthy and strategically located island.

It can be said that the blessings of Sicily – its fertility and its location – were also its curse. Sicily wound up being conquered by the Normans from Northern France in the Middle Ages. The presence of the Normans is attested by many of the religious sites they left, such as the Cathedral of Monreale near Palermo. Such sites are very unique in Italy. Sicily managed an existence as an independent kingdom under Norman and French rule through much of the Middle Ages, though it continued to be fought over. Sicily would, like Naples, eventually fall under the sway of the Aragonese, who would be replaced in the 16th century by the Spanish Habsburgs.

Eventually, Sicily would become a part of the Bourbon Kingdom of the Two Sicilies, which lasted until the Risorgimento. Indeed, Southern Italy was a hotbed of Italian Reunification. The reunification, however, made Sicily into somewhat of an economic backwater, which spurred Sicilians in the hundreds of thousands to leave the island for greener pastures in the United States, Argentina, and elsewhere. Sicily would continue to be somewhat isolated and neglected until the 20th century when it began to experience resurgence as a tourist destination.

Today, Sicilian sites are at the top of tourist destinations in Italy, along with sites in Rome, Tuscany, Venice, and elsewhere. Part of this comes from the handful of tourists who patronized this island in its early years, while others perhaps are inspired by the startlingly real images of the island in movies like *Il Gattopardo* and *The Godfather II*.

Sicily is blessed with beautiful beaches, some of the most picturesque towns in all of Europe, and of course its warm climate. Travelers to Sicily can choose to visit the island alone, or they can work a Sicilian itinerary into travels that include Naples and Rome. There are a large number of sites worth visiting in Sicily so we focused solely on the more notable ones here. Of course, Sicilian beaches are one of a kind, and those will be mentioned separately in a different chapter. Some of the more important Sicilian sites include:

- The Temples of Agrigento
- The Cathedral of Monreale
- The Temples of Selinunte
- Palermo
- Mount Etna
- Syracuse
- Aeolian Islands
- Taormina

The Temples of Agrigento
Sicily is one of the best places in the world to see Greek temples. This is because Sicily was one of the centers of the Magna Graecia, the greater Greek world established by Greek colonization of the Western Mediterranean. The massive temple at Agrigento is one of several important Greek sites in Southern Italy. Although it is a ruin, the temples are in a remarkable state of preservation. There are several temples here, including the Temple of Concordia, the Temple of Juno, the Temple of Olympian Zeus, and the Temple of Hercules. This group has been inscribed in the UNESCO World Heritage List. Be prepared to spend an entire day here.

The Cathedral of Monreale

The Cathedral of Monreale is one of the most important sites of Normal architecture in the world. The Normans were descended from Vikings who settled in France in the Dark Ages. From their power base in Normandy, the Normans were able to expand their influence into other countries like England, which they invaded in 1066, and Sicily, where they reconquered the island from the Saracens and established the Kingdom of Sicily. This church has a very distinct architecture and is well worth a visit.

The Temples of Selinunte

The Temples of Selinunte, like their counterparts in Agrigento, are in a remarkable state of preservation. There are no less than eight temples at this site, dating back to the 6th century BCE and later. Some of these temples exist on an acropolis, a typical structure in Greek towns, which is surrounded by walls of defense. Some of the temples sit on very high ground and are notable for their large columns and air of grandeur.

Palermo

Palermo has long been the capital and most important city of Sicily. Located along the northern coast, Palermo has a number of sites worth visiting, in addition to being a good staging ground for visiting the rest of the island. Palermo contains several notable churches, including the Cappella Palatina and La Martorana (Santa Maria dell'Ammiraglio). Palermo also has the Palermo Archaeological Museum, which contains Greek and Roman finds as well as pre-Greek finds, and, of course, the Cathedral of Monreale is located nearby.

Mount Etna

Many modern tourists like to incorporate natural environmental phenomena into their travels. If you are in this group, then a trip to Mount Etna is for you. Sicily's largest volcano is still active. At approximately 10,000 feet, tourists typically visit a point at about 2500 meters, although skiing does take place near the summit. Mount Etna is located near Taormina and Catania on the eastern side of Sicily, so you can incorporate your visit here to these cities. The region is also known for a long gorge created by the lava flow, the Alcantara Gorge.

Syracuse

Syracuse was in ancient times the most important city of Sicily. Syracuse is still a sizeable city today, making it one of the longest continually inhabited cities in Italy. Syracuse has a number of sites worth visiting, including the Parco Archaeologico della Neapolis. The archaeological park contains a number of ancient Greek and Roman sites, including the Altar of Hiero II, the Roman amphitheater, and the Greek theater.

Aeolian Islands

Southern Italy and Sicily are active volcanic sites, and the Aeolian Islands are no different. The Aeolian Islands are a group of seven volcanic islands located off the northern coast of the island of Sicily. These islands are known for their enchanting coastlines and hot spring. There are also beaches and watersports that make these islands a tourist draw. The Aeolian Islands are typically reached by boat from Messina, off the southern tip of the Italian mainland.

Taormina

Anyone interested in fantastic ancient ruins should also consider a visit to Taormina. This ancient town is known for its beautiful setting. It possesses a Greek theater as well as views of Mount Etna.

Chapter 8: The Best Italian Beaches

Although many tourists come to Italy for Rome, Venice, or Tuscany, some come solely for the beaches. Indeed, like other Mediterranean nations blessed with beaches, like Spain and Greece, Italy often is flooded with tourists in the warm months, tourists who come to partake of the perfect beach weather and surrounds. This is especially true perhaps of tourists from other parts of Europe for whom a trip to Italy or Spain involves a quick jaunt on a train or airplane.

Even if you are a history buff who really wants to visit Italy for the Colosseum, the Uffizi, or Saint Mark's in Venice, there are enough beaches in Italy that it would not be difficult for you to incorporate a trip to one into your itinerary. Indeed, there are so many beaches in Italy that even if you are not a beach nut there is probably a beach out there for you. From the secluded beaches of Sicily and Sardinia to the famous beaches of Italy, Liguria, and Northern Italy, there is a beach out there for everyone.

Of course, the usual advice about beaches holds true for Italian beaches. If you are planning a visit to a beach and intend to go into the water or sit on the sand for a long period of time, you will want to bring a bathing suit, wide-brimmed hat, and, of course, plenty of sunscreens. Do not forget also to bring your wallet, as a beach venture in Italy would not be complete with a glass of wine or ice cream. You also may want to stop for dinner on your way back to the hotel where you are staying.

Although few will have the time to visit all of the beaches on this list, we have provided enough options for most people traveling to Italy. Special attention should be paid to the region of Italy where these beaches are located so that you can determine whether or not this beach or that is actually appropriate in your itinerary. This was all taken into account in the selection of the beaches, so there are selections from the north and the south, as well as the islands of Sicily and Sardinia, blessed with so many beach locales for the natives to enjoy as well as the tourist. Here is our list of the fifteen best beaches in Italy:

- Lido, Venice
- Tropea (Calabria)
- Rimini
- Cefalu (Sicily)
- Viareggio
- Santa Margherita Ligure
- Campo all'Aia (Elba)

- Ischia
- Sanremo
- San Vito Lo Capo (Sicily)
- Capo Testa (Sardinia)
- Costa Sud (Sardinia)
- Otranto
- Camogli (Liguria)
- Cala Goloritze (Sardinia)

Lido

One of the more famous beaches in Italy, the Lido is one of the Venetian beaches and it has been a popular tourist destination since the 1800s. In spite of its fame, travelers to this beach are able to avoid crowds if they come at the right time. This beach is blessed with many amenities, not to mention the many sites of the surrounding Venetian cityscape. The Veneto is also home to many cities that are popular with tourists, so a trip to the Lido can easily be incorporated into a trip that includes Verona, Vicenza, Padua, and the city of Venice itself.

Tropea (Calabria)

Calabria, the toe of the Italian boot, is a region particularly blessed by nature with beaches. This region also has a colorful history, filled with cliff-hugging towns, castles, and great cuisine. Tropea is a town on the Gulf of Saint Euphemia that has been known since Roman times. It was at Tropea that Octavian (later to be known as Augustus) was defeated by Sextus Pompey, the son of Pompey the Great. Tropea is actually sighted on a reef and is connected to the mainland by a strip on which the beach lies. Tropea is well-known for its picturesque setting as well as the other sights in the town and in the surrounding region. A trip to Tropea can easily be incorporated into an itinerary that includes Naples, Sicily, or Southern Italy in general.

Rimini

Rimini is a historic city in Central Italy. Long ruled by the popes, Rimini actually dates from Roman times. In fact, there are many reasons to visit this city, apart from its incredible beach. The city is home to many fabulous churches and great art. Like other places in Italy, Rimini has a quality that makes it easy for tourists to fall in love with the town. But for the purposes of this list, it is the beach at Rimini that is worth note. Indeed, Rimini is blessed with miles of white sand beaches, bathed by the still waters of the Adriatic Sea. As this is a popular beach, you may find it difficult to find a spot in the month of August without booking in advance. This beach may be a little touristy and typical for Italy, but there is a reason why it is so popular. You shall have to come and see for yourself if it is worth the trip. A trip to Rimini can easily be incorporated into an itinerary that includes Rome, Tuscany, and Central Italy.

Cefalu (Sicily)

The city of Cefalu has been known from Phoenician times and the city itself is one of the big draws for tourists to make a stopover at this beach. Indeed, this is a theme of Italian beaches and one that sets Italy apart from other countries with great beaches. The towns and surrounding regions are as much worth a visit as the beach itself. The beach at Cefalu sits below the walled town with its huge cathedral dating from Norman times. Many tourist guidebooks list the Cathedral of Cefalu as one of the top sites in Sicily, wholly apart from the town's beach. Like other Sicilian beaches, you may find less of a horde of tourists here than you might find in North and Central Italy (depending on when you come). This will allow you to enjoy an Italian picturesqueness that it may be hard to find elsewhere. And, of course, there is also the pleasure that comes with a visit to Sicily, one of the unique treasures of Italy.

Viareggio

Viareggio is a spacious beach of beautiful yellow sand, but it is a popular one. Located in Northern Italy, this beach is popular for the denizens of towns like Genoa, Milan, and the Tuscan towns. It is also popular for tourists from other European countries and has been for at least a century. In this regard, Viareggio is classed along with Santa Margherita Ligure and Sanremo, although it does have the character of its own that sets it out apart from the other two. Plan your trip to Viareggio well so that you make sure you get an umbrella.

Santa Margherita Ligure

Liguria is a long stretch of land that was inhabited by the Ligurians in Roman times. These people gave their name to the region, as well as to little towns like Santa Margherita Ligure. Not unlike Sanremo, Santa Margherita Ligure has an old-fashioned flare that may be best-suited for those who like to imagine that they live at different times rather than the present. The gray sand beaches of Santa Margherita Ligure are only steps away from grand hotels that cater to travelers just like you. As it is located in Northern Italy, this beach can be incorporated into a trip to Milan, Lombardy, Genoa, Tuscany, and even Venice.

Campo all'Aia (Elba)

Elba is perhaps best known as the site of exile for French Emperor Napoleon Bonaparte, whose family hailed from nearby Corsica although it was said that they originated from Tuscany. Of course, Napoleon managed to escape from this island to make a second attempt at empire, which led to him being exiled to the much further away Saint Helena. Imperial ambitions aside, it is hard to imagine why anyone would want to escape from this island that teems with wooded beaches and the bluest waters in the Mediterranean. There are many great beaches on the Isle of Elba of which the Campo all'Aia is just one.

In addition to the Campo all'Aia, there is also the spacious Sant'Andrea, the rocky Sansone (considered a good choice for families), and the beaches at Biodola and Forno. A trip to Elba can easily be worked into an Italian vacation centered on Tuscany and Rome. As it is an island, Elba is normally reached by tourists by ferry. The ferries generally leave from the picturesque town of Piombino, which juts out from the rest of Tuscany.

Ischia

Ischia is the beach for you if you plan to visit Naples and Southern Italy. The island of Ischia, on the Bay of Naples, was known for its beaches even in Roman times. The island is actually home to several notable beaches which can be reached by water taxi on this volcanic island. Two of the more well-known beaches include Spiaggia Citara and Spiaggia dei Maronti, which can be incorporated into a travel itinerary that includes Naples, Calabria, and Apulia. And if you would like to visit another nearby island, the smaller island of Procida can also be reached by ferry.

Sanremo

Sanremo is different from this list as it is not a lesser known beach and is only known for achieving notoriety. Sanremo is the Italian Riviera resort par excellence. It was patronized by British, Austrian, and Russian royalty, not to mention the wealthy and the aristocrats from all over Europe in the 19th century. For this reason, Sanremo is a tourist destination completely aside from its beach. The town is filled with Art Nouveau architecture and it has the atmosphere perhaps of a place more sophisticated than the secluded spots of Sardinia or Sicily. You will find here billionaire yacht owners and top hotels. You will have to spend money here, so keep that in mind. Incorporate Sanremo into your tours of Milan, Genoa, and Northern Italy.

San Vito Lo Capo (Sicily)
If going to the beach means to you palm trees and miles and miles of soft white sand and crystal waters, then the beach at San Vito Lo Capo on Sicily may be for you. As a large island in the Mediterranean, Sicily is naturally filled with beaches, some more secluded than others, some more touristy. San Vito Lo Capo cannot be described as secluded as it is a resort, although it is distant from other major tourist sites. It is located near the town of Trapani and is said to resemble the Caribbean more than other beaches in Italy. This makes San Vito Lo Capo an ideal site for tourists from other European countries as well as Americans and others from the Western hemisphere looking for a reminder of home. San Vito is also conveniently located near the Zingaro Nature Reserve. Incorporate San Vito Lo Capo into your travels into Sicily and Southern Italy, although you may want to give yourself a day or two for this stage of your trip.

Capo Testa (Sardinia)

Sardinia may be a lesser known region of Italy, but that is soon to change if the Sardinian beaches have anything to say on the matter. Sardinia is a large island south of Corsica (a part of France) and it has many sights and experiences to attract the traveler. Not least of these are Sardinia's practically untouched beaches. Many of Sardinia's beaches are private, and near the famous Costa Smerelda lies Capo Testa, situated around rocky cliffs and stunning natural scenery. This beach abounds with white sands, although travelers who prefer the more unusual pink sands can easily make a jaunt to the neighboring Maddalena Islands.

Costa Sud (Sardinia)
South of Cagliari, the capital of Sardinia, are numerous beaches. Some lay below hills and coves, while others lie near towns. There are reasons enough to visit Sardinia, but the beaches of Costa Sud and Costa Verde lie near the top of the list. Sardinia is well known for its long and pure beaches, and anyone looking to obtain a unique and less touristy beach experience while getting a flair for the local culture has no further to look than the large island of Sardinia. This beach has five-star hotels as well as other water sporting activities like scuba diving. And it when it comes to the view of the Mediterranean Sea, Sardinia is hard to beat.

Otranto

Located in Southern Italy, Otranto is a picturesque town that has formed the backdrop of many an Italian movie. Located near the very tip of the heel of Italy, in Apulia, Otranto is known for its castle and lighthouse, marking the easternmost area of mainland Italy. The idyllic beach is located near the very end of the Tyrrhenian Sea, where this body of water meets the mass of the Mediterranean. In addition to the beach, travelers to Otranto can stay for the 11th-century cathedral, the catacombs, and for the neighboring Apulian sites, like the town of Lecce which is located nearby.

Camogli (Liguria)
Technically a fishing village, Camogli is also known for its beach, just a short jaunt away from Genoa. A small place of about 5000 people, Camogli was once known for its large fleets of ships, as it is strategically located on the Portofino peninsula. Today, Camogli is an area of a large natural park called the Parco Naturale Regionale di Portofino. This is a unique beach in a town of colorful buildings, and perhaps it is best for those who also want to visit the grand sites of Genoa and the other towns in this northwestern corner of Italy.

Cala Goloritze (Sardinia)

One of the most striking beaches on this list, the Cala Goloritze is located amidst caves, rocky outcroppings, and trees falling perilously into the sea. It is like a beach out of a movie in which a man and woman make love thousands of miles away from any other human beings. If Italy is a country for lovers then Cala Goloritze is the beach for lovers. As the beach is secluded, it is reached by footpath or by boat. Many attempts have been made by the local authorities to keep the beach secluded from the onslaught development, which means that if you have the good fortune to make it here then you are in for a treat. Located in the Ogliastra province of Eastern Sardinia, this beach can be incorporated into tours of Central Italy, Tuscany, and Southern Italy, but plan time for travel here.

Chapter 9: Useful Italian Phrases

It is crucial as a tourist to have some knowledge of Italian if you plan on getting around without an Italian friend to help you. Of course, Italians are used to tourists visiting their nation, but it does help when traveling to show some courtesy by familiarizing yourself with common phrases that can be a great aid in getting around. This will be especially true if you find yourself going off the beaten path in Italy, traveling to places where the people are less likely to come into contact with tourists and probably have less understanding of foreign languages.

As discussed in the introduction and first chapter, Italy is a very diverse country, much more diverse than most people realize, but learning some common phrases in standard Italian will help, even if there may be a local language or dialect in the region of Italy that you are traveling to. Any traveler knows that things like finding the train station, bathroom, or even paying the right price for an item: these things are a whole lot easier if you know a little of the local lingo.

Below is a list of greetings, useful phrases, and days of the week. These are all given to provide basic assistance to travelers in Italy. You may decide to learn more Italian depending on how much time you plan to spend in Italy (or how much time you have to devote to learning a new language). One thing to note about Italian is pronunciation. Emphasis is usually placed on the second to last syllable in the word. So in the word Venezia (the Italian name for Venice), the stress would be placed on the "-ne" rather than the "ve" or the "-zia." *Buona fortuna*!

Greetings:
- **Arrivederci:** Goodbye
- **Buongiorno**: Good morning
- **Buona notte**: Goodnight
- **Buona sera**: Good evening
- **Ciao**: Hello or Goodbye
- **Salve**: Hello
- **Pronto**: Hello (on the phone)

Useful Phrases and Words:
- **Allora**: Therefore or well (transitional word)
- **Bello**: Beautiful
- **Bene, grazie**: Fine, thank you
- **Benvenuto, Benvenuta**: Welcome (to a male, to a female)
- **Buon appetito**: Have a good meal
- **Buona fortuna**: Good luck!

- **Buon viaggio**: Have a good trip
- **Capisce**: Understand?
- **Che ore sono**: What is the time?
- **Chi**: Who?
- **Ci porta il conto**: Would you bring us the bill?
- **Come va**: Where are you?
- **Como si dice in Italiano**: How do you say in Italian?
- **Cosa**: What?
- **Dai**: Come on or really? (exclamation)
- **Dove**: Where? (for directions, for example)
- **Dov'e il bagno**: Where is the bathroom?
- **Dov'e la stazione**: Where is the station?
- **Dov'e la toilette**: Where is the bathroom?
- **Dov'e la metropolitana**: Where is the metro (subway)?
- **Ferma**: Stop!
- **Grazie**: Thank you
- **Grazie tante**: Thank you very much
- **Guarisco presto**: Get well soon
- **Il servizio e incluso**: The tip is included?
- **Mi chiamo**: My name is...
- **Mi dispiace**: I am sorry
- **Mi lasci in pace**: Leave me in peace!
- **Mi puo aiutare**: Can you help me?
- **Mi scusi**: Pardon me, excuse me
- **No**: No
- **Non capisco**: I do not understand
- **Non lo so**: I do not know
- **Non parlo Italiano**: Sorry, I do not speak Italian
- **Non parlo molto bene Italiano**: I do not speak Italian very well
- **Paghera tutto questo signore**: The gentleman will pay for everything
- **Parla inglese**: Do you speak English?
- **Parli piano, per favore**: Please speak slowly
- **Permesso**: Excuse me

- **Perche**: Why?
- **Piacere di conoscerla**: Pleased to meet you
- **Prego**: You are welcome
- **Ripeta, per favore**: Repeat what you said, please
- **Quando**: When?
- **Quanto costa**: How much does it cost?
- **Quanto viene**: How much does the total come to?
- **Salute**: Cheers
- **Scusa**: I'm sorry.
- **Si**: Yes
- **Si, un poco**: Yes, a little
- **Sono**: My name is...
- **Ti amo**: I love you
- **Un cappaccino, per favore**: I would like a cappuccino, please
- **Vuole ballare con me**: Would you like to dance with me?

Days of the Week:
- **Monday**: Lunedi
- **Tuesday**: Martedi
- **Wednesday**: Mercoledi
- **Thursday**: Giovedi
- **Friday**: Venerdi
- **Saturday**: Sabato
- **Sunday**: Domenica

Chapter 10: Cultural Tips: Things Not to Do in Italy

Every country has its unique aspects, which can make traveling there an adventure as well as a potential nightmare. Some degree of cultural confusion is to be expected whenever non-natives travel to out of the way places, but sometimes putting some thought into the sorts of things you do and say, and even how you dress, can go a long way. Naturally, Italians are used to tourists so if you are a not a native they have probably sized you up as such fairly quickly, especially if you are from North America.

Indeed, perhaps one of the biggest travel tips that a kind advisor can give is to try to blend in. This is just as true of Italy as it is of any other country that you might be interested in visiting. It is not so much a question of suppressing your own identity as an attempt at perhaps coming across as less outlandish to the people that live in the country where you are visiting. So wearing a shirt plastered with the American flag on the front with another American flag conveniently placed on the butt of your shorts: sure, you can do that if you want, but do you really want to be that guy?

Of course, Italy is a Western country so it is not as if you are traveling to the Amazon Rainforest or the Congo. Being a slightly obnoxious tourist will not necessarily place you in danger, although you might have a more pleasant experience as a traveler if you try to be agreeable. Again, Italy is a country in Europe so most travelers will have some idea of what is expected of them. Simple things like being courteous, greeting people and saying "thank you," or dressing appropriately can go a long way.

Unique Aspects of Italian Culture
Italy is similar to other European countries, even though it can be said to have an identity all its own. Just like people in all the other countries of the world. Italians are not all the same. Saying that Italians are happy, gregarious people, who enjoy good food and wine may generally be true, but of course, there will be some who do not fit this stereotype.

That being said, Italy is known for the high quality of its food, its fine wine, and the fashion sense of its men and women. Indeed, some of the finest designers of both men's and women's clothes come from Italy, with names like Armani, Fendi, Gucci, Prada, Dolce and Gabbana, Valentino, and Versace being among the more famous although there are many more. If one had to define this as a "unique aspect of Italian culture" one might say that Italians dress well and appropriate to the occasion, and may expect the same from guests. It also has been said that in Italy, as in other Mediterranean countries, the pace of life is somewhat slower so expect to disregard the time once and a while and enjoy a fine glass of red with your new Italian friends.

What Not to Do in Italy

Again, Italy is a European country so the list of dos and don'ts will be similar to that of other nations like Spain, Greece, and France. Like Spain and France, Italy is a Roman Catholic country and that is something that is taken seriously in many places. This means that ladies and gentlemen should put some thought into how they are dressed if they plan on visiting a church, monastery, or other religious sites. This is something to keep in mind as many top destinations in Italy are religious sites so you may want to think about dressing conservatively just in case you may be visiting a church.

For example, a trip to Rome will likely include a stopover in a church so you want to make sure that you are prepared for that. Men will want to wear trousers rather than shorts and shoes rather than sandals. Ladies will also want to wear shoes as well as dresses that fall below the knee. This is a sign of respect for the facility that you are entering as well as the clergy and parishioners who may be at services. One thing that you should do is to tip well (or generously) the people that help you, whether it is the person who served you at the restaurant or the attendant at the hotel. Many European restaurants automatically add the tip in the bill, but if they do not, it is a good idea to be generous rather than tight.

Chapter 11: Travel Tips

There are some basic travel tips that tourists to Italy will want to keep in mind to make their stay a pleasant one. These tips are provided for your convenience, so that you do not end up short of cash, stranded, or in another hairy situation. As mentioned earlier, perhaps the best tip is to plan your trip well in advance. Although playing it by ear is possible in Italy, this will generally mean spending much more money than necessary or potentially missing out on sites that you otherwise would have been able to visit.

Recall that even some beaches in Italy may require a reservation because they can become overwhelmed by visitors at peak times. This is also true for other tourist sites, and, of course, it may also be true of hotels and resorts. In this chapter, we will focus on some of the more significant areas that travelers need to pay attention to, such as currency issues, eating, drinking, and finding a place to stay.

Currency, Eating, and Drinking

The currency of Italy is the Euro, which replaced the Italian lira. Italy shares its currency with several other nations in the European Union, including France and Germany. Although the euro has experienced some fluctuations due to instability issues in the European Union, the euro is consistently stronger than the US dollar: usually valued at between 1.5 times to 2 times the US dollar. Italian hotels, restaurants, and other sites that require payment will generally accept most major credit cards. With that said, it is a good idea to have some cash on hand, even if members of the younger generation feel that cold hard cash is a thing of the past.

As mentioned, most places where you plan to eat or drink will accept cash. This is true of the places mentioned in this book – popular tourist sites like Rome, Milan, Venice, and Florence. In more out of the way areas, you may want to make sure you have some cash with you although you can probably get by with a credit card. If push comes to shove, the attendant at the hotel should be able to point you in the right direction for getting cash. This may be a good time to talk about money changing. Some tourists choose to change their money in their home countries - that is, before they get to Italy – but currency exchange is not always the same depending on where you do the money changing, so you might be better off just doing this in Italy.

Where to Stay

Part of what makes Italy so fun is that there are so many different places to stay. Hotels can even be booked online, which makes for added convenience. This is especially true in larger cities like Rome and Milan, where booking a hotel is not much different from booking one in London, Paris, or New York in this day and age. If you plan on an excursion to an out of the way place, questions of where to stay may require a little more thought. There are really so many options in Italy that just deciding where to stay can be an adventure of its own.

Most tourists choose to stay in hotels with many other tourists, but if you are traveling to a region like Tuscany, Sicily, or even Lombardy, you may want to think about an alternative type of arrangement, like renting an apartment or a villa. This type of arrangement can allow you to have a unique, authentic experience rather than unlike staying in a hotel, which may be just like staying in a hotel in any other country. Depending on how long you plan on staying in Italy, looking into a non-hotel type of stay may be cost-effective. Of course, these types of sites may not allow you to book online so you may have to telephone, although some sites may have an online booking option. Of course, for those looking to save money, there are always hostels. For those able to spend more or traveling with a large group, you may want to look into renting a house or even a castle. One thing to note is that if you book your trip with a travel agent (or as part of a travel tour), your lodgings may already be arranged.

Frequently Asked Questions

1. Why is Italy such a popular tourist destination?

   There are many factors that make Italy an ideal tourist location. Italy's central location near to several European nations has meant that, historically, it was easy for those from other nations to take a quick jaunt over to Italy. Because of Italy's climate and attractions, travelers were attracted to the country, increasing its popularity.

   Italy also benefits from a long history with many monuments to show for it. Indeed, Italy perhaps first became popular as a travel destination for modern times in the 18th century, when noblemen would come to Italy as part of their education. They would already have been educated about the greatness of the Romans, they would have read Roman poets and writers, and a stopover in Italy would have been part of their education. This legacy of Italy as a tourist destination began then but persists to today. Finally, as beach culture has become prominent in the West since the 19th century, Italy is an obvious choice because of all of its beaches.

2. Is there something about Italy that makes it different from other countries in Europe?

   There are a few things that make Italy unique. Italy's geography and location have meant that this nation was the target of migrations and invasions since before recorded history. Indeed, there are monuments so old, clearly from pre-Roman and pre-Etruscan times, that archaeologists can only speculate on who built them.

Historians are not even sure where the Etruscans or the Romans themselves came from.

What is unique about this is that it means that Italian history is filled with interesting, unanswered questions. Also, the people of Italy today probably represent sort of a living record of the many different peoples that passed through here. Although most countries in Europe can attest to a complex ethnohistory, perhaps few have such long-lasting heterogeneity, with the monuments to match, as Italy. When it is also remembered that Italy did not become a unified nation until 1861, another unique aspect appears.

3. Is there anything about Italy that tourists should know?

Tourists should know that Italy is a country that has manages to have both a national character and to be diverse at the same time. There are differences between Northern and Southern Italy for example, but there are even differences between Milan and Venice in the North or between Apulia and Calabria in the South. Everywhere you go you will find different cuisines, local wines, and frequently local languages and dialects.

What the tourist should keep in mind is that learning some Italian phrases can help, but that there might be places where Italian is less useful, such as rural parts of Sardinia or Sicily for example. Also, tourists should remember that Italy is essentially a Roman Catholic country, so they might want to be a little more conservative in their dress when visiting religious sites, especially in the Vatican.

4. Are there areas in Italy that are must-sees that all travelers should go to?

Every tourist has their own sense of what drew them to visit that particular country or region. Some tourists may choose to visit a place because their family originated there or because their favorite film took place there. Others may choose a destination because it is known for the high quality of its beaches. When it comes to a country like Italy, there really is no wrong reason to visit.

That being said, tourists to Italy would really be remiss if they did not take in a few prominent sites. Because Italy is a long, narrow nation, the traveler can be faced with whether they should focus their travels on the North or the South. Fortunately, Rome is in the center so an itinerary that focuses on Rome can easily become part of a Northern or Southern journey, depending on your interests. We would argue that the monuments of Rome, such as the Colosseum, Vatican, and Roman Forum are must-sees in Italy, but one could just as easily argue for the museums of Florence or the Grand Canal in Venice.

5. What are the best beaches in Italy?

As a nation with an incredibly long coastline, there are many incredible beaches in Italy. Indeed, the Italian nation is also blessed with many islands, and arguably many of the best beaches are located on these. Although there is not a consensus of what the best beaches in Italy are, travel guides do tend to agree on what makes a good beach. The best beaches will be sites of stunning beauty, clean and clear blue waters, and ideally something less than the usual horde of tourists that Italy is often inundated with. There also some beaches, like those in Venice or the Italian Riviera that are famous, and this may help to garner them a place on the list.

Some of the beaches on this list will be in regions of Italy that are less visited, such as the island of Sardinia. We did not have time to discuss Sardinia thoroughly on this list but this island, like Sicily, is unique in the existence of a language and other cultural aspects that are quite distinct from other parts of Italy. Although you may not be coming to Italy specifically for the beaches, it may be a good idea to incorporate a beach into your itinerary just to say that you have been there. With that out of the way, here is our list of the 15 best beaches in Italy:

- Lido, Venice
- Tropea (Calabria)
- Rimini
- Cefalu (Sicily)
- Viareggio
- Santa Margherita Ligure
- Campo all'Aia (Elba)
- Ischia
- Sanremo
- San Vito Lo Capo (Sicily)
- Capo Testa (Sardinia)
- Costa Sud (Sardinia)
- Otranto
- Camogli (Liguria)
- Cala Goloritze (Sardinia)

6. Can I get by in Italy with a basic knowledge of common Italian phrases?

   Although Italy historically had a dozen or so regional languages, today people in most parts of Italy can speak and understand standard Italian. There are more isolated areas of Italy where it may be helpful to learn some phrases in the local language or dialect, but travelers heading to most areas covered in this book should be able to get by with the phrases covered in this book.

The traveler should also keep in mind that many Italians have familiarity with other languages like English so even if you have not completely mastered the list of common phrases you should still be able to get by. Italy receives millions of tourists from all over the world every year and they are well equipped to help travelers on their way. No tourist to Italy is expected to master the Italian language before they come although it does help.

7. Is Italian culture different from mainstream European culture (if there is such a thing)?

There are many distinct aspects of Italy, which stem from Italy's unique history. As we have mentioned, several languages are spoken in Italy in addition to Italian, and there is a wide range of geographic differences, variations in cuisine and local traditions wherever you go in Italy. That being said, Italy is a part of Europe and there is overlap between Italian culture and the local cultures of other European countries.

For example, as a Mediterranean country, Italy has some aspects of its cuisine that reflect its climate and close position of the sea. But Greece and Spain are also European countries so there are some basic similarities in cuisine across these countries. Another area of commonality is language. Italian is a Romance language that is similar to other languages derived from Latin like Spanish. Italy is also a Roman Catholic country with traditions similar to other Catholic nations of Europe in some ways.

8. How much money should I bring to Italy?

This will all depend on where you go in Italy, how long you plan to stay, and other factors. Like other Western European nations, Italy can be quite expensive, especially if you are heading to popular tourist areas like Rome, Milan, or Florence. Indeed, European travel has a reputation for being costly compared to travel to other parts of the world. Tourists should be prepared to have cash on hand for dining out and getting around in addition to expenses that they have already paid for hotels, flights, et cetera.

Although Italy can be quite expensive, there are ways that tourists can save money. Booking inexpensive hotels online far ahead of time is an easy way to save money. Of course, this requires knowing your itinerary far in advance. Also, traveling during off-peak times can help, especially if you are going to a popular beach or other sites that are space limited and tend to become packed with tourists.

9. Why does Italy have such a long tradition of art and culture compared to other European countries?

Italy's location has allowed it to receive influences from neighboring regions even dating back to ancient times. The Romans were influenced by groups like the Etruscans and Greeks in their early history, and later by other groups like the Egyptians and Persians from whom they learned the worship of Near Eastern gods. What this means is that culture in Italy was honed to a high state of sophistication because of these diverse influences.

In the late Middle Ages and Renaissance, the situation was quite different. Italy was a center of religious art during this time, and the artists of this period were more culturally isolated perhaps than Italians in ancient times because this period was not particularly notable for a high state of culture. Italian artists, therefore, had to get the creative ball rolling again, a feat which they accomplished quite successfully. How were they able to do this? Well, you will have to travel to Italy to find out.

10. Who were the condotierri?

This is the name given to the army leaders and warlords who rose in Italy during the late Middle Ages. Although Northern Italy was technically part of the Germanic Holy Roman Empire, Italy was actually divided into petty territories and city-states that were ruled by local rulers, often known as podesta. The condotierri would be hired by states to lead their armies, and many rose to become rulers in their own right, such as the Sforza in Milan and the Riario in Forli. These men were important because their legacy lies in the many strong castles, churches, and lavish art that is especially common in Northern Italy.

11. Is the Vatican part of Italy?

Technically, the Vatican is not part of Italy. The Vatican is a sovereign state located entirely within the city of Rome. The Vatican is one of the smallest countries in the world, consisting of the many church buildings and museums that lie around St. Peter's Church. But the Vatican was once the center of a large state known as the Papal States that was suppressed during the Italian Reunification. Today, the Vatican can easily be visited in your tour of Rome.

12. Should I integrate Italy into a wider European vacation or is it better to make Italy a trip onto itself?

Because there is so much to see, most people decide to focus their travels solely on Italy, although it is certainly possible to incorporate Italy into a larger European vacation. Italy is a long and narrow country, so there can be some travel time reaching other nations, especially if you are in Southern Italy. That being said, Italy is still close to other major tourist nations like France, Spain, Greece, and Croatia, so the dedicated traveler can certainly find ways to incorporate Italy into a broader Mediterranean vacation if that is their goal.

13. When is the best time to visit Italy?

Many travelers to Italy plan to spend a lot of time outdoors so the ideal time would be the summer months. Although travel during this time can be done and has been done many people also plan to go to Italy at this time so you may deal with large crowds, higher than normal prices, or even sites that may be completely booked. Indeed, some popular beaches may have not even a couple of feet of spare sand for you to lie on in the dead of summer.

For this reason, some choose to visit Italy at other times of the year. Italy's warm climate permits travel during much of the year. Depending on where you would like to go, a vacation in the fall or even early winter may be an idea.

14. Is Italian a difficult language to learn?

Italian is a Romance language similar to Spanish. Indeed, it may be relatively easy for travelers to learn some Italian if they already know Spanish. But even if you have not studied another Romance language or Latin, it is not difficult to pick up some Italian. Basic phrases will help you get around without incident, although in many cities local people will have some familiarity with English.

15. Is it safe for tourists in Italy?

It is perfectly safe for tourists at the vast majority of sites in Italy. Italy is like most other countries that receive large numbers of tourists. Most areas are very safe, although some areas may be more prone to crime than others. Basic common sense travel advice applies in Italy just as it would apply somewhere else. Be more careful at night. Be more careful in places where there are fewer tourists. Try to blend in if you can. It is always a good idea to be less flashy and conspicuous while traveling, especially in out of the way areas.

Conclusion

Few countries in the world have the allure of Italy. Although there are other countries that can boast about the same number of tourist visits a year or about the same degree of traveler dollars spent, few places leave such an indelible impression as Italy. This is a country that travelers visit and return year after year. One of the reasons why visitors return is because it is nearly impossible to see everything that there is to see in this fantastic country in one trip, but also because there is an air to Italy that keeps travelers coming back again and again.

Indeed, even the Romans recognized that there was something special Italy, a characteristic that they tended to attribute to the greatness of their own city. Some Romans believe that the secret name of Rome, or Roma in Latin, was Amor, the letters of "Roma" spelled backward. Rome was the city of Venus just as much as it was the city of Jupiter, and perhaps, it is in establishing a mood for love that Italy manages to trump its tourist competitors.

Many tourists come to Italy to see Rome, but they often stay for the host of other sites that characterize the country. Rome is just one of the many cities in Italy that are worth visiting. It is easy to understand why Rome is a popular tourist destination. Let's face it. There is no city in the world quite like Rome. Even the layout of Rome with its seven hills and its parks strewn with villas and monuments is strange and wonderful. A trip to Rome is like a trip back in time. There is something essentially un-modern about Rome and most tourists find that delightful.

If it is ancient monuments that one is interested in, these can be found all over Italy. Of course, it is difficult for other Italian cities to match Rome with its Colosseum, Palatine Hill, and Baths of Caracalla and Diocletian, but even smaller Italian cities often have a Roman archway, a Roman-era section of wall, or a Roman temple or theater. As we have seen, Sicily and Southern Italy have not only Roman ruins, but Greek ones, making Italy literally a museum of ancient civilizations like no other.

And the Italian cultural immersion does not stop with ancient sites. Christian religious sites are just as numerous and elaborate as the Roman and Greek sites are. In fact, few countries in Europe have such a record of church buildings of varied architectural styles as Italy. In Milan and Lombardy, as well as Rome, church buildings from the very beginning of the Christian period can be found. Of course, extravagant churches of the Renaissance and Baroque period can also be found. All of this makes Italy an art lovers dream.

Naturally, some travelers would rather visit Italy for the beaches. If that is your goal, you will find that you are basically traveling to a nation filled with beaches. Italy's shape and geography, right in the middle of the Mediterranean, means that the options are endless for the beachgoer looking for the perfect beach to plant their towel and umbrella on. From the trendy beach resorts of Northern Italy to the secluded picturesque beaches of Sicily and Sardinia, the traveler will find themselves inundated with beach hopping options. Indeed, there are so many beautiful beaches here that you can easily find that you have spent your entire vacation on the beach.

What this means for most travelers is that a trip to Italy must be followed by another. This is just as true today as it was in the 18th-century when tourists from Northern Europe would find themselves returning to Italy again and again. Although they were primarily drawn by the profusion of artistic and architectural sites, these early travelers must have recognized that even the beaches of Italy were without peer.

Beaches and architectural sites join forces with Italian wine and cuisine to make Italy into a unique touristic experience. How many countries can say that their food and wine is even better than their artistic sites? Italy is really a place like no other. Of course, this means that it is very easy to spend a lot of money in Italy, especially if you find yourself transforming your vacation into a stay twice as long as you originally planned. Italy is also pricy because of the large number of well-heeled tourists who come here, although there are savvy travelers who manage to enjoy the country on a shoestring budget.

There are important tips to keep in mind when you are visiting Italy. It may help to get a handle on the language so that you can get around with ease in some of the less touristy areas. It is also important to respect the local culture in terms of being a little more covered up when you visit places like the Vatican or perhaps making a point not to be too underdressed, as being dressed appropriately is something that the people of this land tend to notice.

But the big question for most travelers is how they will manage to see all that there is to see in Italy in so short a time. Perhaps that is why so many people come to Italy and never leave. With careful planning, you can make the most of your Italian adventure. And whatever you do not manage to see this year can always be left for next.

See you soon in Italy!

Made in the USA
Middletown, DE
03 December 2019

79922342R00062